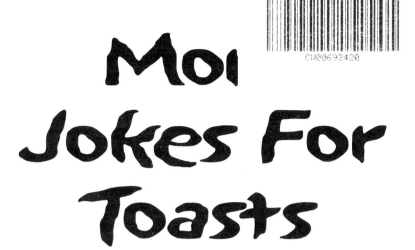

More Jokes For Toasts

Jack Bright

Lewis Masonic

First published 2004

ISBN 0 85318 236 1

Published by Lewis Masonic

an imprint of Ian Allan Publishing Ltd, Hersham, Surrey KT12 4RG.
Printed by Ian Allan Printing Ltd, Hersham, Surrey KT12 4RG.

Dear Reader,

Previous volumes of *Jokes for Toasts* have been masonically slanted.

It meant that using the jokes for any other organisation required manipulation of words or phrases.

To save the reader having to do this, in this volume I have omitted the masonic ties. There are also a large number of jokes that are just simply jokes.

Some are men-only. Some are for the ladies and some general. Some are one-liners and throwaway remarks!

So . . . Read, Use and Enjoy.

Pete and Larry had not seen each other in many years. Now they had a long talk trying to fill in the gap of those years by telling about their lives.

Finally Pete invited Larry to visit him in his new apartment.

'I've got a wife and three kids and I'd love to have you visit us.'

'Great. Where do you live?'

'Here's the address. And there's plenty of parking behind the apartment. Park and come around to the front door, kick it open with your foot, go to the lift and press the button with your left elbow, then enter! When you reach the sixth floor, go down the hall until you see my name on the door. Then press the doorbell with your right elbow and I'll let you in.'

'Good. But tell me . . . what is all this business of kicking the front door open, then pressing buttons with my left then my right elbow?'

'Surely you're not coming empty-handed!'

*****

On New Year's Eve the Master of Ceremonies stood up in the bar and said that it was time to get ready. At the stroke of midnight, he wanted everybody to be standing next to the one person who made his life worth living.

Well, it was embarrassing. The barman was almost crushed to death.

*****

At the airport counter, a woman was complaining about the departure time, saying: 'Young man, I could stick a feather in my rear and get there faster.'

The assistant smiled and said: 'Madam, all runways are cleared for take-off!'

Here is a story from America about people shovelling the snow to make a parking space in front of their house. This apparently is a problem for the police in Chicago every winter. What happens is that somebody will park in a nearby car park, then slave away for however many hours it takes to shovel out a car-sized space in front of his house, naturally, so that he can park his car there. Then he goes back to the car park to get his car.

When he returns home, he finds that the space has been taken by some other car. He is, to put it mildly, upset.

What most people do is to write nasty notes etc and place them on the windscreen of the offending vehicle. Where the police get involved, however, is in the occasional case where the individual vents his wrath in somewhat more violent means. Tyres and throats have been slashed over this.

Once somebody got creative. Instead of doing the usual nasty stuff, he got out his garden hose and watered the car down, really well. I mean, very, very thoroughly. The water, of course, froze solid. When the owner returned, instead of a car, he found a car-sized ice lolly.

The note on the car read: 'You want the space? Here, it's yours until spring!'

*****

A gentleman entered a busy florist shop that displayed a large sign that read: 'Say It With Flowers'.

'Wrap up one rose,' he told the florist.

'Only one?' the florist asked.

'Just one,' the customer replied. 'I'm a man of few words.'

Another story from America: It is Saturday morning as Jake, an avid hunter, wakes up ready to bag the first deer of the season. He walks down to the kitchen to get a cup of coffee, and to his surprise he finds his wife, Alice, sitting there, fully dressed in camouflage.

Jake asks her: 'What are you up to?'

Alice smiles: 'I'm going hunting with you!'

Jake, though he has many reservations about this, reluctantly decides to take her along. Later they arrive at the hunting site. Jake sets his wife safely up in the tree stand and tells her: 'If you see a deer, take careful aim at it and I'll come running back as soon as I hear the shot.'

Jake walks away with a smile on his face knowing that Alice couldn't bag an elephant — much less a deer. Not 10 minutes pass when he is startled as he hears a fusillade of gunshots.

Quickly, Jake starts running back. As Jake gets closer to her stand, he hears Alice screaming: 'Get away from my deer!'

Confused, Jake races faster towards his screaming wife. And again he hears her yell: 'Get away from my deer!' followed by another volley of gunfire.

Now within sight of where he had left his wife, Jake is surprised to see a cowboy, with his hands high in the air. The cowboy, obviously distraught, says: 'Okay, lady, okay!!!! You can have your deer!!! Just let me get my saddle off it!'

*****

A Sunday school teacher asked her little children, as they were on the way to the church service: 'And why is it necessary to be quiet in church?'

One bright little girl replied: 'Because people are sleeping.'

During the wedding rehearsal, the groom approached the vicar with an unusual offer. 'Look, I'll give you £100 if you'll change the wedding vows. When you get to me and the part where I'm to promise to "love, honour and obey" and "forsaking all others, be faithful to her forever", I'd appreciate it if you'd just leave that part out.' He passed the minister two £50 notes and walked away satisfied.

It is now the day of the wedding, and the bride and groom have moved to that part of the ceremony where the vows are exchanged. When it is time for the groom's vows, the vicar looks the young man in the eye and says:

'Will you promise to prostrate yourself before her, obey her every command and wish, serve her breakfast in bed every morning of your life and swear eternally before God and your lovely wife that you will not ever even look at another woman, as long as you both shall live?' The groom gulps and looks around, and says in a tiny voice: 'Yes.'

The groom leans toward the vicar and hisses: 'I thought we had a deal.'

The vicar puts the £100 into his hand and whispers back: 'She made me a much better offer.'

*****

Our office discussions somehow turned to charging hookers on our company credit card (I claim innocence). The obvious problem is getting the expense account cleared with 'Hooker' as an item.

We noticed through repeated arduous trials that the local strip club (the French Maid) showed up as 'French Restaurant', and decided hookers would be worth a try. But what would they discreetly call themselves?

'Laptop servicing', of course.

A nun was sitting at a window in her convent one day when she was handed a letter from home. Upon opening it a £10 note dropped out. She was most pleased at receiving the gift from her relatives, but as she read the letter her attention was distracted by the actions of a shabbily dressed stranger who was leaning against a post in front of the convent.

She couldn't get him off her mind and, thinking that he might be in financial difficulties, she took the £10 and wrapped it in a piece of paper, on which she had written: 'Don't despair, Sister Mercy' and threw it out of the window to him. He picked it up, read it, looked at her with a puzzled expression, tipped his hat and went off down the street.

The next day she was in her cell saying her rosary when she was told that a man was at the door who insisted on seeing her.

She went down and found the shabbily dressed stranger waiting for her. Without saying a word he handed her a roll of banknotes. When she asked what they were for he replied: 'That's the £60 you are owed. Don't Despair came in at 5-1.'

*****

Childhood: That time of life when you make funny faces in the mirror.

Adulthood: That time of life when the mirror makes funny faces back.

*****

A man is a person who will pay £2 for a £1 item he wants. A woman will pay £1 for a £2 item that she doesn't want.

A man was sitting in the doctor's waiting room, and said to himself every so often: 'Lord, I hope I'm sick!'

After about the fifth or sixth time, the receptionist couldn't stand it any longer and asked: 'Why in the world would you want to be sick, Mr Adams?'

The man replied: 'I'd hate to be well and feel like this.'

*****

A computer programmer was crossing the road one day when a frog called out to him and said: 'If you kiss me, I'll turn into a beautiful princess.'

He bent over, picked up the frog and put it in his pocket. The frog spoke up again and said: 'If you kiss me and turn me back into a beautiful princess, I will stay with you for one week.'

The computer programmer took the frog out of his pocket, smiled at it and returned it to the pocket. The frog then cried out, 'If you kiss me and turn me back into a princess, I'll stay with you and do ANYTHING you want.'

Again the computer programmer took the frog out, smiled at it and put it back into his pocket.

Finally, the frog asked: 'What is the matter? I've told you I'm a beautiful princess, that I'll stay with you for a week and do anything you want. Why won't you kiss me?'

The computer programmer said: 'Look, I'm a computer programmer. I don't have time for a girlfriend, but a talking frog, now that's cool.'

*****

Two stockbrokers went to lunch. One looked at the other and said: 'Let's relax while we eat and talk about something other than the market or any kind of business at all.'

'Good idea, Sam. Let's talk about women.'

'OK — common or preferred?'

There was once an aspiring veterinary surgeon who put himself through veterinary college working nights as a taxidermist.

Upon graduation, he decided he could combine his two vocations to serve better the needs of his patients and their owners, while doubling his practice and, therefore, his income.

He opened his own surgery with a sign on the door saying: 'Dr Jones, Veterinary Medicine and Taxidermy — Either way, you get your dog back!'

*****

At a chemist's, a blonde woman asked to use the infant scale to weigh the baby she held in her arms. The assistant explained that the machine was being repaired, but said that she would calculate the child's weight by weighing the woman and baby together on the adult scale, then weighing the mother alone and subtracting the second amount from the first.

'It won't work,' countered the woman. 'I'm not the mother, I'm the aunt.'

*****

One day a sweet little girl becomes puzzled about her origin.

'How did I get here, Mummy?' she asks.

Her mother replies, using a well-worn phrase: 'Why, God sent you, darling.'

'And did God send you too, Mummy?' she continues.

'Yes, sweetheart, he did.'

'And Daddy, and Grandma and Grandpa, and their mummies and daddies, too?'

'Yes, dear, all of them, too.'

The child shakes her head in disbelief. 'Then you're telling me there's been no sex in this family for over 200 years? No wonder everyone is so grouchy!'

A few nights ago a few friends and I were in a pub, telling all the Irish jokes we knew. Anyway, I ducked into the gents for the usual. While I was in there, this big fellow came in and said to me: 'Hey, mate, I'm Irish and I don't like you telling all those Irish jokes.'

So I said: 'Well, they're not against you, just against anyone in Ireland.'

'My mother is in Ireland!' he screamed, and pulled out a razor.

Was I scared! I am sure he would have killed me if he had found somewhere to plug it in!

*****

A young naval officer had nearly completed his first overseas tour of sea duty when he was given an opportunity to display his ability at getting the ship under way. With a stream of crisp commands, he had the decks buzzing with men and soon the ship had left port and was steaming out of the channel.

The young officer's efficiency had been remarkable. In fact, the deck was abuzz with talk that he had set a new record for getting a destroyer under way. He glowed at his accomplishment and was not at all surprised when another seaman approached him with a message from the captain.

He was, however, a bit surprised to find that it was a radio message, and he was even more surprised when he read: 'My personal congratulations upon completing your underway preparation exercise according to the book and with amazing speed. In your haste, however, you have overlooked one of the unwritten rules — make sure the captain is aboard before getting under way.'

BE ON THE LOOK-OUT FOR THE FOLLOWING COMPUTER VIRUSES:

VIAGRA VIRUS

Makes a new hard drive out of an old floppy.

RONALD REAGAN VIRUS

Saves your data, but forgets where it is stored.

MIKE TYSON VIRUS

Quits after two bytes.

OPRAH WINFREY VIRUS

Your 300MB hard drive suddenly shrinks to 100MB, then slowly expands to 200MB.

DISNEY VIRUS

Everything in your computer goes Goofy.

PROZAC VIRUS

Screws up your RAM but your processor doesn't care.

ARNOLD SCHWARZENEGGER VIRUS

Terminates some files, leaves, but IT WILL BE BAAAAACK.

IDIOTS AT WORK . . .

I was signing the receipt for my credit card purchase when the shop assistant noticed that I had never signed my name on the back of the credit card. She informed me that she could not complete the transaction unless the card was signed. When I asked why, she explained that it was necessary to compare the signature on the credit card with the signature I just signed on the receipt. So I signed the credit card in front of her. She carefully compared that signature to the one I signed on the receipt. As luck would have it, they matched.

ADVICE FOR IDIOTS

An actual tip from page 16 of the 'Environmental Health & Safety Handbook for Employees' (American of course): 'Blink your eyelids periodically to lubricate your eyes.'

IDIOTS IN THE NEIGHBOURHOOD

I live in a semi-rural area near to the New Forest. We recently had a new neighbour call the local council offices to request the removal of the 'Deer Crossing' sign on our road. The reason: many deer were being hit by cars and he no longer wanted them to cross there.

IDIOTS IN FOOD SERVICE

My daughter went to a local Taco Bell and ordered a taco. She asked the individual behind the counter for 'minimal lettuce'.

He said he was sorry, but they only had iceberg.

IDIOT SIGHTINGS . . .

Sighting 1:

I was at the airport, checking in at the gate, when the airport employee asked: 'Has anyone put anything in your baggage without your knowledge?'

I said: 'If it was without my knowledge, how would I know?'

He smiled and nodded knowingly: 'That's why we ask.'

Sighting 2:

The pedestrian crossing on the corner emits a beeping sound when it is safe to cross the road. I was crossing with an intellectually challenged work colleague of mine, when she asked if I knew what the beeping sound was for. I explained that it signals to blind people when the light is red.

She responded, appalled: 'What on earth are blind people doing driving?'!!

Sighting 3:

At a good-bye lunch for an old and dear work colleague who was leaving the company due to 'downsizing', our manager spoke up and said: 'This is fun. We should have lunch like this more often.' Not another word was spoken. We just looked at each other like rabbits staring into the headlights of an approaching lorry.

Sighting 4:

I worked with an individual who plugged her extension cable back into its plug and for the life of her could not understand why her system would not turn on.

Sighting 5:

When my husband and I arrived at a car showroom to pick up our car, we were told that the keys had been accidentally locked in it. We went to the service department and found a mechanic working feverishly to unlock the driver's-side door. As I watched from the passenger's side, I instinctively tried the door handle and discovered it was open. 'Excuse me,' I said to the mechanic, 'it's open!'

'I know,' answered the young man, 'I've already done that side.'

*****

A little girl and a little boy are at nursery one day. The girl approaches the boy and says: 'Hey, Tommy, do you want to play house?'

He says: 'All right. What do you want me to do?'

The girl replies: 'I want you to communicate your thoughts.'

'Communicate my thoughts?' says a bewildered Tommy. 'I have no idea what that means.'

The little girl smirks and says: 'Perfect. You can be the husband.'

*****

The Western Australian police have just launched a new unit that roves around dealing with trouble spots. It was launched on New Year's Eve with an assignment to control crowds at a large concert; it made the TV news, with an officer proudly saying they were the: Police 'Fast Action Response Team'.

Oh dear. What an acronym.

A vicar wanted to raise money for his church, and being told there was a fortune to be made in horse racing, he decided to purchase a horse and enter it in the races. However, at the local auction, the going price for horses was so high that the vicar decided to buy a donkey instead. To his great surprise, the donkey did quite well and came in third place. The next day, the racing paper carried this headline:

'Vicar Shows Ass'

The vicar was so pleased with the donkey that he entered it in the races again, and this time the animal won first place. The paper said:

'Vicar's Ass Out In Front'

The bishop was so upset with this kind of publicity that he ordered the vicar not to enter the donkey in any more races. The newspaper printed this headline:

'Bishop Scratches Vicar's Ass'

This was too much for the bishop and he ordered the vicar to get rid of the donkey. The vicar decided to give the animal to a nun in a local convent. The next day, the headlines read:

'Nun Has Best Ass In Town'

The bishop fainted. When he came around, he informed the nun that she would have to dispose of the donkey. The nun searched, finally finding a farmer willing to buy the animal for £10. The paper stated:

'Nun Peddles Ass for £10!'

They buried the bishop the next day.

A little boy at nursery school was sitting at his desk making funny faces at anyone who would watch.

The teacher came by and saw what he was doing and said calmly: 'Billy, you had better stop doing that, your face might get stuck that way.'

Billy stared back just as calmly and said in reply: 'You must have learned the hard way.'

*****

A man walks into a car spares and says: 'I'd like a rear view mirror for my Skoda.'

The man behind the counter thinks about this for a while, then says: 'OK, seems like a fair swap to me.'

*****

A wife asks her husband: 'Darling, if I died, would you remarry?'

'After a considerable period of grieving, I suppose I would. We all need companionship.'

'If I died and you remarried,' the wife asks, 'would she live in this house?'

'We've spent a lot of money getting this house just the way we want it. I'm not going to get rid of my house. I suppose she would.'

'If I died and you remarried, and she lived in this house,' the wife asks, 'would she sleep in our bed?'

'Well, the bed is brand new, and it cost us £1,000. It's going to last a long time, so I suppose she would.'

'If I died and you remarried, and she lived in this house and slept in our bed, would she use my golf clubs?'

'Oh, no,' the husband replies. 'She's left-handed.'

After a two-week criminal trial in a very high-profile bank robbery case, the judge turns to the jury foreman and asks: 'Has the jury reached a verdict in this case?'

'Yes, we have, Your Honour,' the foreman responds.

'Would you please pass it to me,' the judge declares, as he motions for the court attendant to retrieve the verdict slip from the foreman and deliver it to him.

After the judge reads the verdict himself, he delivers the verdict slip back to the attendant to be returned to the foreman and instructs the foreman: 'Please read your verdict to the court.'

'We find the defendant Not Guilty of all four counts of bank robbery', states the foreman. The family and friends of the defendant jump for joy at the verdict and hug each other as they shout expressions of divine gratitude.

The man's lawyer turns to his client and asks: 'So, what do you think about that?'

The defendant, with a bewildered look on his face, then turns to his lawyer and says: 'I'm confused here. Does this mean that I have to give all the money back?'

*****

A man goes into a petrol station to fill his car with petrol. The petrol overflows and goes up his arm.

He pays for the fuel and starts to drive away. As he hits the road he lowers his window and lights a cigarette.

Whoosh — his arm is engulfed in flames. He sticks it out of the window and waves it about to try to put out the flames.

A passing police car stops him and they wrap a cloth round the flames and put the fire out.

Two days later he receives a summons for carrying a firearm!!

An elderly couple had a son who was still living with them. The parents were a little worried, as the son was still unable to decide about his future career, so they decided to do a small test. They took a £10 note, a Bible and a bottle of whisky, and put them on the front hall table . . . then they hid, pretending they were not at home. The parents' plan was: 'If our son takes the money, he will be a businessman, if he takes the Bible, he will be a priest — but if he takes the bottle of whisky, I'm afraid our son will be a drunkard.' So the parents hid in the nearby cupboard and waited nervously. Peeping through the keyhole they saw their son arrive . . . The son saw the money they had left. He took the £10 note, looked at it against the light, and slid it in his pocket. After that, he picked up the Bible, flicked through it, and took it. Finally he grabbed the bottle, opened it, and took an appreciative sniff to be assured of the quality . . . then he left for his room, carrying all three items. The father slapped his forehead, and said: 'It's even worse than I could ever have imagined . . . Our son is going to be a politician!'

*****

My parents have been married for 50 years. I asked my mother how they did it. She said: 'You just close your eyes and pretend it's not happening.'

*****

I went out with this girl for two years and then the nagging started: 'I want to know your name, I want to know your name, I want to know . . .'

In a small country pub, all the patrons became quite used to the landlord's little dog being around the pub, so were quite upset when one day the little dog died.

Everyone met to decide how they could remember the little dog. The decision was made to cut off his tail and stick it up behind the bar to remind everyone of the little dog's wagging tail.

The little dog went up to Heaven and was about to run through the pearly gates when he was stopped by Saint Peter, who questioned the little dog as to where he was going.

The little dog said: 'I have been a good dog — so I am going into Heaven where I belong!'

Saint Peter replied: 'Heaven is a place of perfection; you cannot come into Heaven without a tail. Where is your tail?'

The little dog explained what had happened back on earth.

St Peter told the little dog to go back down to earth and retrieve his tail. The little dog protested that it was now the middle of the night on earth, but St Peter would not change his mind.

So the little dog went back down to earth and scratched on the door of the pub until the landlord who lived upstairs came down and opened the door.

'My goodness, it is the spirit of the little dog. What can I do for you?' said the landlord.

The little dog explained that he wasn't allowed into Heaven without his tail, and he needed it back. The landlord replied: 'I would really like to help you, but my drinks licence doesn't allow me to serve spirits after hours!'

*****

Love is like an hourglass, with the heart filling up as the brain empties.

This man goes up to a woman in a pub and said: 'Hey, honey, can I buy you a drink?' She said: 'No, but I'll take the £2.20 instead.'

*****

If love is the answer, can you rephrase the question?

*****

The difference between being in a relationship and being in prison is that in prisons they let you play softball at the weekends.

*****

Love is an exploding cigar which we willingly smoke.

*****

A lot of people wonder how you know you're in love. Just ask yourself this one question: 'Would I mind being financially destroyed by this person?'

*****

I joined a local singles group. The other day the secretary called me up and said: 'Welcome to the group. I want to find out what kind of activity you like to plan.'

I said: 'Well, weddings.'

Marriage is a wonderful institution, but who wants to live in an institution?

*****

I don't think of myself as single. I'm just romantically challenged.

*****

A hesitant driver, waiting for a traffic jam to clear, came to a complete stop at a road junction.

The traffic thinned, but the driver still waited.

Finally a furious voice from the vehicle behind him cried: 'The sign says "Give Way", not "Give up"!'

*****

A vicar gave a talk to the local sports club on sex. When he got home, he couldn't tell his wife that he had spoken on sex, so he said he had discussed horseback riding with the members.

A few days later, she bumped into some men at the shopping centre and they complimented her on the speech her husband had made.

She said: 'Yes, I heard. I was surprised about the subject matter, as he's only tried it twice. The first time he got so sore he could hardly walk, and the second time he fell off.'

Morris walks into an insurance office and asks for a job.

'We don't need anyone,' he is told.

'You can't afford not to hire me,' Morris says. 'I can sell anyone, anytime, anything!'

'Well, we have two policies that NO ONE has been able to sell. If you can sell just one, you have a job.'

He is gone about two hours. He returns and hands them two cheques, one for £25,000 and another for £50,000.

'How in the world did you do that?' they ask.

'I told you I'm the world's best salesman,' Morris says. 'I can sell anything, anywhere, anytime!'

'Did you get a urine sample?' they ask.

'What's that?' he asks.

'Well, if you sell a policy over £20,000, the company requires a urine sample. Take these two bottles and go back and get urine samples.'

Morris is gone about six hours, and they are getting ready to close when in he walks with two five-gallon buckets, one in each hand. He sets the buckets down, reaches in his shirt pocket and produces two bottles of urine. He sets them on the desk and says: 'Here's Mr Brown's and this one is Mr Smith's.'

'That's good,' they say, 'but what's in those two buckets?'

'Well, I passed by the Holiday Inn and they were having a Ladies' Festival, so I stopped and sold them a group policy!'

*****

The first woman recruit in the Army reported for duty and was told that although her quarters would be in a separate building, she was to mess with the men.

It wasn't until four weeks later someone finally told her that meant to eat her meals with them.

A hurricane blew across the Caribbean towards America. It didn't take long for the expensive yacht to be swamped by high waves, sinking without a trace. There were only two survivors: the boat's owner Dr Eskin and its steward Benny who both managed to swim to the closest island.

After reaching the deserted strip of land, the steward was crying and very upset that they would never be found. The other man was quite calm, relaxing against a tree.

'Dr Eskin, Dr Eskin, how can you be so calm?' cried Benny. 'We're going to die on this lonely island. We'll never be discovered here.'

'Sit down and listen to what I have to say, Benny,' began the confident Dr Eskin. 'Five years ago I gave the Grand Charity £10,000 and another £10,000 to the Appeal. I donated the same amounts four years ago. And, three years ago, since I did very well in the stock market, I contributed £15,000 to each. Last year business was good, so the two charities each got £20,000.'

'So what?' shouted Benny.

'Well, it's time for their annual fund drives, and I know they're going to find me,' smiled Dr Eskin.

*****

My friend Ken told me when he was in the Navy he used to use this 'drill' while he was the bridge watch:

'Now this is a drill, this is a drill! All hands forward lay aft! All hands aft lay forward! All hands starboard lay port! All hands port lay starboard! All hands above decks lay below decks! All hands below decks lay above! All hands amidships stand by to collect casualties and direct traffic! This is a drill!'

With deep concern, Dick noted that his friend Conrad was far drunker than he'd ever seen him before. He walked over to the bar and asked: 'What's the trouble, mate?'

'It's a woman,' replied Conrad. 'What else?'

'Tell me about it,' coaxed Dick.

'It's your wife.'

'My wife? What about her?'

'Well, my friend, I'm afraid she's cheating on us.'

*****

Our lager,
Which art in barrels,
Hallowed be thy drink.
Thy will be drunk (I will be drunk),
At home as in the tavern.
Give us this day our foamy head,
And forgive us our spillages,
As we forgive those, who spill against us.
And lead us not to incarceration,
But deliver us from hangovers.
For thine is the beer,
The bitter and the lager.
Forever and ever,
. . .

*****

Q: How did the blonde woman injure herself raking leaves?

A: She fell out of the tree.

The idiot sightings continue (all true):

Some Boeing employees on the airfield decided to steal a life raft from one of the 747s. They were successful in getting it out of the plane and taking it home. When they took it for a float on the river, they were surprised by a coastguard helicopter coming towards them. It turned out that the chopper was homing in on the emergency locator that is activated when the raft is inflated. Needless to say, they are no longer employed there!

*****

A husband and wife are having dinner at a very fine restaurant when this absolutely stunning young woman comes over to their table, gives the husband a big kiss, tells him she'll see him later, and walks away.

His wife glares at him and says: 'Who was that??!!'

'Oh,' replies the husband, 'that was my mistress.'

The wife says, 'That's it; I want a divorce.'

'I understand,' replies her husband, 'but, remember, if you get a divorce, there will be no more shopping trips to Paris, no wintering in the Caribbean, no Lexus in the garage, and no more country club. But the decision is yours.'

Just then the wife notices a mutual friend entering the restaurant with a gorgeous woman. 'Who's that woman with Jim?' she asks.

'That's his mistress,' replies her husband.

'Ours is prettier,' says the wife.

A girl asks her boyfriend to come over Friday night and have dinner with her parents. Since this is such a big event, the girl announces to her boyfriend that after dinner she would like to go out and make love for the first time.

Well, the boy is ecstatic, but he has never had sex before, so he takes a trip to the chemist shop to get some condoms. The pharmacist helps the boy for about an hour. He tells the boy everything there is to know about condoms and sex. At the register, the pharmacist asks the boy how many condoms he'd like to buy: a three-pack, 10-pack or a family pack.

'I'm really going to put it to this girl,' the boy tells the pharmacist. 'I really don't know but I'm sure it's going to last a long time.'

The pharmacist, with a laugh, suggests the family pack, saying the boy will be rather busy, it being his first time and everything.

That night, the boy shows up at the girl's parents' house and meets his girlfriend at the door. 'Oh, I'm so excited for you to meet my parents, come on in!' The boy goes inside and is taken to the dinner table where the girl's parents are seated. The boy quickly offers to say grace and bows his head.

A minute passes, and the boy is still deep in prayer with his head down. Ten minutes pass, and still no movement from the boy. Finally, after 20 minutes with his head down, the girlfriend leans over and whispers to the boyfriend: 'I had no idea you were this religious.'

The boy turns, and whispers back: 'I had no idea your father was a pharmacist.'

Two rednecks, LeRoy and Earl, were driving down the road in the American Deep South drinking a couple of bottles of Bud.

The passenger, LeRoy, said: 'Lookey thar up ahead, Earl, it's a po-lice roadblock! We're gonna get busted fer drinkin' these here beers!!'

'Don't worry, LeRoy,' Earl said. 'We'll just pull over and finish drinkin' these beers, peel off the label and stick it on our foreheads, and throw the bottles under the seat.'

'What fer?' asked LeRoy.

'Just let me do the talkin', OK?' said Earl.

Well, they finished their beers, threw the empty bottles under the seat, and each put a label on their foreheads.

When they reached the roadblock, the sheriff said: 'You boys been drinkin'?'

'No sir,' Earl said. 'We're wearin' a patch.'

*****

As an elderly man was driving down the motorway, his car phone rang.

Answering, he heard his wife's voice urgently warning him: 'Harold, I just heard on the news that there's a car going the wrong way on the M6. Please be careful!'

'It's not just one car,' said Harold. 'There's hundreds of them!!!'

*****

A drunkard goes to the doctor complaining of tiredness and headaches. 'I feel tired all the time, my head hurts, I've got a sore bum, and I'm not sleeping. What is it, doctor?'

The doctor examines him thoroughly and says: 'I can't find anything wrong. It must be the drinking.'

'Fair enough,' replies the drunkard. 'I'll come back when you sober up.'

A Hampshire man stops by a café for breakfast. After paying the bill, he checks his pockets and leaves his tip — three pence.

As he strides toward the door, his waitress muses, only half to herself: 'You know, you can tell a lot about a man by the tip he leaves.'

The man turns around, curiosity getting the better of him. 'Oh, really? Tell me, what does my tip say?'

'Well, this penny tells me you're a thrifty man.' Barely able to conceal his pride, the man utters, 'Hmm, true enough.'

'And this penny, it tells me you're a bachelor.' Surprised at her perception, he says, 'Well, that's true, too.'

'And the third penny tells me that your father was one, as well.'

*****

A man was brought to a Mercy Hospital in the States, and went in for coronary surgery. The operation went well, and as the groggy man regained consciousness he was reassured by a Sister of Mercy waiting by his bed. 'Mr Smith, you're going to be just fine,' the nun said while patting his hand. 'We do have to know, however, how you intend to pay for your stay here. Are you covered by insurance?'

'No, I'm not,' the man whispered hoarsely.

'Can you pay in cash?'

'I'm afraid I can't, Sister.'

'Do you have any close relatives, then?'

'Just my sister in New Mexico,' he replied, 'but she's a spinster nun.'

'Nuns are not spinsters, Mr Smith,' the nun replied. 'They are married to God.'

'Okay,' the man said with a smile, 'then send the bill to my brother-in-law.'

A mother and baby camel are talking one day when the baby camel asks: 'Mummy, why have I got these huge three-toed feet?'

The mother replies: 'Well, son, when we trek across the desert, your toes will help you to stay on top of the soft sand.'

A few minutes later, the young camel asks: 'Mummy, why have I got these long eyelashes?'

'They are there to keep the sand out of your eyes on the trips through the desert.'

'Mummy, why have I got these great big humps on my back?'

'They are there to help us store water for our long treks across the desert, so we can go without drinking for long periods.'

'So, we have huge feet to stop us from sinking, long eyelashes to keep the sand out of our eyes and these humps to store water.'

'Yes, dear.'

'So why are we in London Zoo?'

*****

Two teenagers were arrested for public lewdness and possession of marijuana when they were found naked, each smoking a joint, sitting on the edge of the fountain in the town square.

The arresting officer told them they were entitled to a phone call, since he was unable to contact either parent.

Some time later, a man entered the police station and the sergeant said: 'I suppose you're the children's lawyer.'

'No,' the man replied. 'I'm just here to deliver them a pizza.'

For all of you out there who've had to deal with an irate customer, this one is for you. It's a classic! In tribute to those 'special' customers we all love! An award should go to the British Airways gate agent at Heathrow for being clever and funny, and making her point, when confronted with a passenger who probably deserved to fly as cargo:

A crowded BA flight was cancelled. A single agent was rebooking a long queue of inconvenienced travellers. Suddenly an angry passenger pushed his way to the desk. He slapped his ticket down on the counter and said, 'I HAVE to be on this flight and it has to be FIRST CLASS.'

The agent replied: 'I'm sorry, sir. I'll be happy to try to help you, but I've got to help these people first, and I'm sure we'll be able to work something out. Please take your turn in the queue.'

The passenger was unimpressed. He asked loudly, so that the passengers behind him could hear: 'Do you have any idea who I am?'

Without hesitating, the gate agent smiled and grabbed her public address microphone. 'May I have your attention, please?' she began, her voice bellowing throughout the terminal. 'We have a passenger here at the gate WHO DOES NOT KNOW WHO HE IS. If anyone can help him find his identity, please come to the gate.'

With the folks behind him in line laughing hysterically, the man glared at the BA agent, gritted his teeth and swore: 'Screw you!'

Without flinching, she smiled and said: 'I'm sorry, sir, but you'll have to stand in the queue for that, too.'

A man who had problems with premature ejaculation went to a sex shop for a cure. The assistant handed him a little yellow can and said: 'This is Stay-Hard Spray; put on a little and you can go all night!'

Delighted, the man took it home, put it on the cellar shelf and waited eagerly for bedtime, when he sprayed some . . . and went upstairs to his wife.

But it seemed to make him reach orgasm quicker than ever. The next day he returned to the sex shop, slammed the can down on the counter, and snapped: 'This stuff makes me worse than before!'

Reading the label, the assistant asked: 'Did you hide the stuff on your cellar shelf?'

'Yes, so?' said the disgruntled customer.

'You must have grabbed the wrong can. This is WD 40.'

*****

I've just got some junk mail from this organisation that wants me to save the forest. I sent them back a letter saying stop sending me the junk mail and save the forest yourself.

*****

The following list of phrases and their definitions might help you to understand the mysterious language of science and medicine. These special phrases are also applicable to anyone reading a PhD thesis or academic paper:

'IT HAS LONG BEEN KNOWN' . . . I didn't look up the original reference.

'A DEFINITE TREND IS EVIDENT' . . . This data is practically meaningless.

'WHILE IT HAS NOT BEEN POSSIBLE TO PROVIDE DEFINITE ANSWERS TO THE QUESTIONS' . . . An unsuccessful experiment, but I still hope to get this paper published.

'THREE OF THE SAMPLES WERE CHOSEN FOR DETAILED STUDY' . . . The other results didn't make any sense.

'TYPICAL RESULTS ARE SHOWN' . . . This is the prettiest graph.

'THESE RESULTS WILL BE IN A SUBSEQUENT REPORT' . . . I might get around to this sometime, if pushed/funded.

'IN MY EXPERIENCE' . . . Once.

'IN CASE AFTER CASE' . . . Twice.

'IN A SERIES OF CASES' . . . Thrice

'IT IS BELIEVED THAT' . . . I think.

'IT IS GENERALLY BELIEVED THAT' . . . A couple of others think so, too.

'CORRECT WITHIN AN ORDER OF MAGNITUDE' . . . Wrong.

'ACCORDING TO STATISTICAL ANALYSIS' . . . Rumour has it.

'A STATISTICALLY-ORIENTED PROJECTION OF THE SIGNIFICANCE OF THESE FINDINGS' . . . A wild guess.

'A CAREFUL ANALYSIS OF OBTAINABLE DATA' . . . Three pages of notes were obliterated when I knocked over a beer glass.

'IT IS CLEAR THAT MUCH ADDITIONAL WORK WILL BE REQUIRED BEFORE A COMPLETE UNDERSTANDING OF THIS PHENOMENON OCCURS' . . . I don't understand it.

'AFTER ADDITIONAL STUDY BY MY COLLEAGUES' . . . They don't understand it either.

'THANKS ARE DUE TO JOE BLOGGS FOR ASSISTANCE WITH THE EXPERIMENT AND TO CINDY ADAMS FOR VALUABLE DISCUSSIONS' . . . Mr Bloggs did the work and Ms Adams explained to me what it meant.

'A HIGHLY SIGNIFICANT AREA FOR EXPLORATORY STUDY' . . . A totally useless topic selected by my committee.

'IT IS HOPED THAT THIS STUDY WILL STIMULATE FURTHER INVESTIGATION IN THIS FIELD' . . . I quit.

*****

There's a new toy on the market called the Billy doll. It's being advertised as the first openly gay doll for sale. And the doll is anatomically correct.

That doll must be sending Barbie mad, don't you think?

Finally a male doll with something 'down there', and he turns out to be gay. Isn't that every woman's nightmare?

One snowy Saturday, Ted was having a coffee with his friend Roger, a bus driver. 'What's new at the bus depot, Roger?'

'I got a commendation the other day.'

'Congratulations. What did you do?' Ted asked.

'Well, on Tuesday, just after the start of my first run of the day, a drunk got on the bus and fell asleep. After watching people avoid the seats near the drunk for one and a half circuits of my route, I finally took the man and dragged him off the bus.'

Ted was shocked. 'You got a commendation for throwing a poor drunk off the bus and into the snow?'

'No, no,' Roger replied. 'On my next run I noticed the drunk was still lying in the snow so I dragged him back into the warmth of the bus. Someone saw me do that and phoned the office up.'

*****

A mother was preparing pancakes for her sons, Kevin, five, and Ryan, three. The boys began to argue over who would get the first pancake.

Their mother saw the opportunity for a moral lesson. 'If Jesus were sitting here, He would say: "Let my brother have the first pancake. I can wait."'

Kevin turned to his younger brother and said: 'Ryan, you be Jesus!'

A big-city lawyer was representing the railway in a lawsuit filed by an old farmer. The farmer's prize bull was missing from the field through which the railway passed. The farmer only wanted to be paid the fair value of the bull.

The case was scheduled to be tried before the local JP. The city-slicker lawyer for the railway immediately cornered the farmer and tried to get him to settle out of court.

He did his best selling job, and finally the farmer agreed to take half of what he was asking.

After the farmer had signed the release and taken the cheque, the young lawyer couldn't resist gloating a little over his success, telling the farmer: 'You are really a country hick, old man, but I put one over on you in there. I couldn't have won the case. The driver had fallen asleep when the train went through your field that morning. I didn't have one witness to put on the stand. I bluffed you!'

The old farmer replied: 'Well, I'll tell you, young man, I was a bit worried about winning that case myself, because that bull came home this morning.'

*****

In this particular branch of the Army's officer training college, the instructor was returning a test. The students identified their work by the last four digits of their Army number. In the early hours of a morning, the instructor was calling the numbers.

'Four-seven-seven-zero?' he asked.

'Here,' replied one half-awake lieutenant-to-be. Taking the paper, though, he realised he had mistakenly asked for the wrong paper.

'Seven-zero-seven-five?' asked the instructor.

'Here,' repeated the student, gearing for trouble.

'I thought you were four-seven-seven-zero, soldier,' said the teacher.

'That's right, sir,' answered our hero. 'I have a nick-number.'

Old Andrzej was a minister in a small Polish town. He had always been a good man and lived by the Bible. One day God decided to reward him, allowing him the answer to any three questions Andrzej would like to ask.

Old Andrzej did not need much time to consider, and the first question was: 'Will there ever be married Catholic priests?'

God promptly replied: 'Not in your lifetime.'

Andrzej thought for a while, and then came up with the second question: 'What about female priests then, will we have that one day?'

Again God had to disappoint old Andrzej: 'Not in your lifetime, I'm afraid.'

Andrzej was sorry to hear that, and he decided to drop the subject. After having thought for a while, he asked the last question: 'Will there ever be another Polish pope?'

God answered quickly and with a firm voice: 'Not in My lifetime.'

*****

'Tell me something,' asked John, 'how many cakes can you eat on an empty stomach, Arthur?'

Arthur scratched his head and said: 'Well, five, I think.'

'Wrong,' said John. 'You can only eat just one. After that, your stomach isn't empty any more! Gotcha!'

Arthur was impressed so he decided to try the joke on his wife, Jenny, when he got home.

'Hey, darling, how many cakes can you eat on an empty stomach?'

Jenny thought for a minute or two (it takes awhile to get those two brain cells to fire together) and said: 'Two.'

Arthur was dejected. 'Oh, if you'd said "FIVE" I had a GREAT joke for you!'

A very good-looking man walks into a singles bar, gets a drink and sits down. During the course of the evening he tries to chat with every single woman who walks into the bar, with no luck.

Suddenly a really ugly man, and I mean a R-E-A-L-L-Y ugly man, walks into the bar. He sits at the bar, and within seconds he is surrounded by women. Very soon he walks out of the bar with two of the most beautiful women you ever saw.

Disheartened by all this, the good-looking man asks the barman: 'Excuse me, but that really ugly man just came in here and left with those two stunning women — what's his secret? He's as ugly as sin and I'm everything a girl could want but have not been able to pull all night. What's going on?'

'Well,' said the barman, 'I don't know how he does it, but he does the same thing every night. He walks in, orders a drink, and just sits there licking his eyebrows . . .'

*****

Eagles may soar, but weasels don't get sucked into jet engines.

*****

The early bird gets the worm, but the second mouse gets the cheese.

*****

Ambition is a poor excuse for not having enough sense to be lazy.

A man in America went to an department store last week to buy Valentine's cards for his daughter and mother. The 50ft of displays for hundreds of cards astounded him. He muttered out loud: 'I wonder if they have cards for ex-spouses.'

The assistant behind the counter said: 'Oh, yes sir, we do have an "ex" category, but they're in Sporting Goods.'

'Really?'

'Yes, sir. They're called bullets.'

*****

I was on a flight about a year ago. The cabin crew were going through the safety announcement and were talking about the masks that come out of the overhead locker. The attendant said: 'In the event you are seated next to a child, ensure that you put on your mask first and then assist the child with their mask. But only if they've been good.'

*****

A woman was complaining to the neighbour that her husband always came home late, no matter how much she complained.

'Take my advice,' said the neighbour, 'and do what I did. Once my husband came home at three o'clock in the morning, and from my bed, I called out, "Is that you, Jim?" And that cured him.'

'Cured him?' asked the woman. 'But how?'

The neighbour said: 'You see, his name is Bill.'

A young boy answers the phone.
A man says: 'Hello, is your dad around?'
The boy whispers: 'Yes.'
The man then asks if he can talk to him.
'He's busy at the moment,' the boy whispers.
'Then is your Mummy there?'
'Yes,' the boy whispers.
'Can I talk to her?'
'No, she's busy,' the boy whispers.
'Is there anyone else there?'
'Yes,' whispers the boy.
'Who?' the man asks.
'A policeman,' comes the whispered reply.
'Well, can I talk to him?'
'He's busy too,' the boy whispers.
'Is there anyone else there then?'
'Yes,' whispers the boy.
'Who then?' the man asked.
'A fireman,' the boy whispers.
'Can I talk to him?'
'No,' the boy whispers, 'he's busy.'
Annoyed, the man asks what they are all doing.
'Looking for me,' the boy whispers.

*****

Linda and Marion were comparing notes on the difficulties of running a small business. 'I started a new practice last year,' Linda said. 'I insist that each of my employees takes at least a week off every three months.'

  'Why in the world would you do that?' Marion asked.

  'It's the best way I know of to learn which ones I can do without,' Linda said.

GOOD: A policeman had a perfect spot to watch for speeding motorists, but wasn't catching many. Then, he discovered the problem — a 10-year-old boy was standing up the road with a hand-painted sign that read 'RADAR TRAP AHEAD'. The officer then found a young accomplice down the road with a sign reading 'TIPS' and a bucket full of change.

BETTER: A motorist was sent a picture of his car speeding past a speed camera. A £60 speeding fine was included. Being cute, he sent the police department a picture of £60. The police responded with another photo in the post — of handcuffs.

BEST: (A true story) A young woman was pulled over for speeding. As the motorcycle officer walked to her car window, flipping open his ticket book, she said: 'I bet you are going to sell me a ticket to the Traffic Policemen's Ball.' He replied: 'Traffic policemen don't have balls.' There was a moment of silence while she smiled, and he realised what he'd just said.

He then closed his book, got back on his motorcycle and left. She was laughing too hard to start her car for several minutes.

*****

Paddy O'Shea came over from Ireland and got friendly with some of the local Irish in London, and they took him to an upmarket 'Irish' pub.

'Amazin', just amazin', that's what London is,' he said, looking with delight into his glass. 'Never have I been seein' an ice cube with a hole in it!'

'Oi sure have,' said his host, Michael Sullivan. 'Bin married to one fer 15 year.'

Three priests and a rabbi were sitting together on a train, getting comfortable for a three-hour journey.

After 20 minutes the first priest said: 'I have something to confess and I can only tell fellow clerics like you. I only work on Sundays and therefore I have three bottles of whisky delivered each week. I drink one on Monday, spend Tuesday in bed ill, drink another Wednesday and spend Thursday in bed ill, and I drink the third on Friday and spend Saturday in bed ill . . . now I've confessed I feel better.'

The second priest said: 'I would like to confess. The donations that are made to the church, I have been keeping, and twice a year I go to Las Vegas . . . now I've confessed I feel better.'

The third priest said: 'I too have a confession! There is a beautiful nun in the convent next door and — well, you know — we are men of the world with normal passions . . . now I've confessed I feel better.'

There was a few moments' silence, then the Rabbi said: 'Gentlemen, I too have a weakness — I am a terrible gossip and just can't wait to get off this train.'

*****

'Hey! This looks like a great meal! I knew my partner had a beautiful wife,' said Ray, 'but I didn't know you were a fantastic cook as well.'

'I feel I should warn you, Ray,' she simpered, 'that I expect my husband home in an hour.'

'But I'm not doing anything,' he protested.

'I know,' she sighed. 'I just wanted to let you know how much time you had.'

Memo to head office:

To ensure that you have a good time on your trip to Australia, your team members have planned and developed a special itinerary to fill your free time. Agenda follows:

Day 1: The '10 Deadliest Snakes' Autumn Tour. You and a guest will be escorted through the outback and provided with the opportunity to handle and examine each of the world's 10 most deadly snakes.

Day 2: The 'Great White Encounter'. You and your tour guide will take a small boat to the Great Barrier Reef, where you will be able to dive into the fishbait-laden water and experience the beauty of the Great White Shark.

Day 3: The Aboriginal 'Festival of Spears'. You will be the honoured guest of a small Aboriginal village as it celebrates the subjugation of the Aboriginal race by the white man, with free drink and a special weapons exhibition.

Day 4: The 'Crocodile Dundee' Petting Zoo. You will be able to come up close to the occasionally harmless salt-water crocodiles of the Australian coast. Lucky spectators are asked to participate in a croc-wrestling exhibition.

Day 5: 'Those Marvellous Moray Eels'. This tour will once again return you to the beauty of the Great Barrier Reef, where you will be allowed to hand-feed special finger-shaped sausages to the wild eels of Stubby Hand Reef.

We hope you will enjoy your trip!
Your loyal employees.

Two gas company servicemen, a senior training supervisor and a young trainee were out checking meters on a housing estate. They parked their van at one end of an alleyway and worked their way to the other end.

At the last house a woman looking out of her kitchen window watched the two men as they checked her building's gas meter.

After they had checked the meter, the senior supervisor challenged his younger colleague to a race down the alleyway back to the van to prove that an older man could outrun a younger one.

As they came running up to the van, they realised the woman from that last house was huffing and puffing right behind them.

They stopped and asked her what was wrong.

Gasping for breath, she replied: 'When I saw two gasmen running as hard as you two were, I thought I'd better run too!'

*****

A lady is walking down the street to work and she sees a parrot in a pet shop. The parrot says to her: 'Hey lady, you are really ugly.'

Well, the lady is furious! And she storms past the shop to her work. On the way home she sees the same parrot in the window and the parrot says to her: 'Hey lady, you are really ugly.'

She is incredibly angry now. The next day she sees the same parrot and the parrot says to her: 'Hey lady, you are really ugly.'

The lady is so furious that she goes into the shop and says that she will sue the shop and kill the bird. The manager says: 'That's not good,' and promises the bird won't say it again.

When the lady walks past the shop after work the parrot says to her: 'Hey lady.' She pauses and says: 'Yes?' and the bird says: 'You know.'

Did you hear about the disaster at a leading university?

The scientists were cloning monkeys and one of them blew up.

The scientists are trying to determine what went wrong by sifting through the rhesus's pieces.

*****

The congregation liked its new vicar, but was somewhat puzzled by his speaking style. His first sermon ran only eight minutes; the second Sunday he spoke for 45 minutes; the third week he rattled on for an hour-and-a-half.

That was enough for the Board to summon him for a little chat.

To their relief, the clergyman had a ready explanation. 'The Saturday before the first sermon, I had my teeth pulled and my mouth was still terribly sore. But, by the time a week had gone by, I'd got used to my new dentures.'

Here the vicar paused, and blushed deeply. 'And as for last Sunday, well, I'm afraid that I picked up my wife's set of teeth by mistake!'

*****

True story: I was on a flight from London to Glasgow, when the steward announced:

'Good afternoon. Welcome aboard flight 437 London Heathrow to Glasgow. For our snack this afternoon you will enjoy the choice of peanuts, peanuts, or peanuts. Parents, please be advised that all screaming children must be stored in the overhead bins.'

Memo No 1:
With immediate effect, the company is adopting Fridays as Casual Day so that employees may express their individuality.

Memo No 2:
Spandex and leather micro-miniskirts are not appropriate attire for Casual Day. Neither are string ties, rodeo belt buckles or moccasins.

Memo No 3:
Casual Day refers to dress only, not attitude. When planning Friday's wardrobe, remember image is a key to our success.

Memo No 4:
A seminar on how to dress for Casual Day will be held at 4pm Friday in the cafeteria. Fashion show to follow.
Attendance is compulsory.

Memo No 5:
As a result of Friday's seminar, the Committee Of Committees has appointed a 14-member Casual Day Task Force to prepare guidelines for proper dress.

Memo No 6:
The Casual Day Task Force has completed a 30-page manual. A copy of 'Relaxing Dress Without Relaxing Company Standards' has been sent to each employee. Please read the chapter 'You Are What You Wear' and consult the 'home casual' versus 'business casual' checklist before leaving for work each Friday. If you have doubts about the appropriateness of an item of clothing, contact your CDTF representative before 7am on Friday.

Memo No 7:
Because of lack of participation, Casual Day has been discontinued, with immediate effect.

A couple of weeks ago I gave to my six children and their families a list of some presents I would like to have from 'Old Santa'. One of the items listed was a belt, waist 48-50 (I am of ample proportions). The following is a true story told to me by my son-in-law, Jack, last night.

He and my seven-year-old grandson, John, were out looking at presents last week and my son-in-law told John to go and look for a belt — size 48-50. A little later John came back with the longest belt he found (size 44). Jack told him to take it back and get one 48-50.

John came back a second time, again with the largest belt he could find (size 46). Jack told him again to get a size 48-50! Whereupon John asked: 'Dad, do they really make cows that long?'

*****

'That wife of mine is a liar,' said the angry husband to a sympathetic friend sitting next to him in the pub.

'How do you know?' the friend asked.

'She didn't come home last night and when I asked her where she'd been, she said she had spent the night with her sister, Shirley.'

'So?'

'So she's a liar. I spent the night with her sister Shirley.'

*****

Did you know that dolphins are so intelligent that within only a few weeks of captivity, they can train humans to stand at the edge of the pool and throw them fish?

One girl to another: 'I got a sweater for Christmas. I wanted a screamer or a moaner.'

*****

A blonde went to the electrical shop sale and found a bargain.
'I would like to buy this TV,' she told the salesman.
'Sorry, we don't sell to blondes,' he replied.
She hurried home and dyed her hair, then came back and again told the salesman: 'I would like to buy this TV.'
'Sorry, we don't sell to blondes,' he replied.
Damn, he recognised me, she thought. She went for a complete disguise this time, haircut and new colour, new outfit, big sunglasses, then waited a few days before she again approached the salesman: 'I would like to buy this TV.'
'Sorry, we don't sell to blondes,' he replied.
Frustrated, she exclaimed: 'How do you know I'm a blonde?'
'Because that's a microwave,' he replied.

*****

A teacher in an art class asked his students to sketch a naked man. As the teacher walked around the class checking the sketches, he noticed that one of the young ladies had sketched the man with an erection.
The teacher said: 'Oh, no, I wanted it the other way.'
She replied: 'What other way???'

- 48 -

An elderly couple were visiting London's Covent Garden when the wife noticed her husband staring at the trendy young women in their short skirts and revealing tops.

'Henry,' his wife said, 'stop that! You look like you've never seen a woman's legs or breasts before!'

'You know,' he replied somewhat sadly, 'I was just thinking the exact same thing myself.'

*****

Reaching the end of a job interview, the interviewer asked a young engineer fresh out of university: 'And what starting salary were you looking for?'

The engineer said: 'Around £45,000 a year, depending on the benefits package.'

The interviewer said: 'Well, what would you say to a package of five weeks holiday, 14 paid holidays, full medical and dental care, a company-matching retirement fund to 50% of salary, and a company car leased every two years, say, a red Ferrari?'

The engineer sat up straight and said: 'Wow! Are you joking?'

And the interviewer replied: 'Yes, but you started it.'

*****

Tennis is like marrying for money. Love has nothing to do with it.

Why does Sea World have a seafood restaurant? I'm halfway through my fishburger and I realise: 'Oh, my God — I could be eating a slow learner!'

*****

An atheist was spending a quiet day fishing when suddenly his boat was attacked by the Loch Ness monster. In one easy flip, the beast tossed him and his boat at least a hundred feet into the air. The monster then opened its mouth while waiting below to swallow man and boat.

As the man sailed head over heels and started to fall towards the open jaws of the ferocious beast he cried out: 'Oh, my God! Help me!'

Suddenly, the scene froze in place. As the atheist hung in mid-air, a booming voice came out of the clouds and said: 'I thought you didn't believe in Me!'

'God, come on, give me a break!' the man pleaded. 'Just seconds ago I didn't believe in the Loch Ness monster either!'

'Well,' said God, 'now that you are a believer you must understand that I won't work miracles to snatch you from certain death in the jaws of the monster, but I can change hearts. What would you have me do?'

The atheist thought for a minute and then said: 'God, please have the Loch Ness monster believe in You also.' God replied: 'So be it.'

The scene started in motion again with the atheist falling towards the ravenous jaws of the ferocious beast.

Then the Loch Ness monster folded his claws together and said: 'Lord, bless this food You have so graciously provided…'

Why are our days numbered and not, say, lettered?

*****

Oh, friends are just enemies who don't have enough guts to kill you.

*****

John bought two horses, and could never remember which was which. A neighbour suggested that he cut the tail of one horse and that worked well until the other horse got his tail caught in a bush. It tore so that it looked exactly like the other horse's tail and our friend was stuck again.

The neighbour suggested that John notch the ear of one horse. That worked well until the other horse caught his ear on a barbed wire fence. Once again our friend couldn't tell them apart.

The neighbour suggested he measure the horses for height.

When he did, he was very pleased to find that the white horse was 2 inches taller than the black.

*****

There is report of a two-seater private plane which crashed into a large cemetery in Ireland.

The Irish Fire Department has reported recovering over 300 bodies and is still digging . . .

Actual signs seen:

Sign in a launderette:
AUTOMATIC WASHING MACHINES: PLEASE REMOVE
ALL YOUR CLOTHES WHEN THE LIGHT GOES OUT

In an office:
WOULD THE PERSON WHO TOOK THE STEP LADDER
YESTERDAY PLEASE BRING IT BACK OR FURTHER
STEPS WILL BE TAKEN

Outside a photographer's studio:
OUT TO LUNCH: IF NOT BACK BY FIVE, OUT FOR
DINNER ALSO

Notice sent to residents of a Wiltshire village:
DUE TO INCREASING PROBLEMS WITH LITTER LOUTS
AND VANDALS WE MUST ASK ANYONE WITH
RELATIVES BURIED IN THE GRAVEYARD TO DO THEIR
BEST TO KEEP THEM IN ORDER

Outside a second-hand shop:
WE EXCHANGE ANYTHING — BICYCLES, WASHING
MACHINES ETC. WHY NOT BRING YOUR WIFE ALONG
AND GET A WONDERFUL BARGAIN?

Sign outside a new town hall which was to be opened by the
Prince of Wales:
THE TOWN HALL IS CLOSED UNTIL OPENING. IT WILL
REMAIN CLOSED AFTER BEING OPENED. OPEN
TOMORROW

Outside a disco:
SMART'S IS THE MOST EXCLUSIVE DISCO IN TOWN.
EVERYONE WELCOME

Sign warning of quicksand:
QUICKSAND. ANY PERSON PASSING THIS POINT WILL
BE DROWNED. BY ORDER OF THE DISTRICT COUNCIL

Notice in a dry-cleaner's window:
ANYONE LEAVING THEIR GARMENTS HERE FOR
MORE THAN 30 DAYS WILL BE DISPOSED OF

Notice in a health food shop window:
CLOSED DUE TO ILLNESS

Spotted in a safari park:
ELEPHANTS PLEASE STAY IN YOUR CAR

Seen during a conference:
FOR ANYONE WHO HAS CHILDREN AND DOESN'T
KNOW IT, THERE IS A DAY CARE ON THE FIRST FLOOR

Notice in a field:
THE FARMER ALLOWS WALKERS TO CROSS THE
FIELD FOR FREE, BUT THE BULL CHARGES

Sign on a repair shop door:
WE CAN REPAIR ANYTHING. (PLEASE KNOCK HARD
ON THE DOOR — THE BELL DOESN'T WORK)

Spotted in a toilet in a London office block:
TOILET OUT OF ORDER. PLEASE USE FLOOR BELOW

The Department of Health is considering additional warnings on beer and other alcohol bottles, such as:

WARNING: consumption of alcohol may make you think you are whispering when you are not.

WARNING: consumption of alcohol is a major factor in dancing like an idiot.

WARNING: consumption of alcohol may cause you to tell the same boring story over and over again until your friends want to SMASH YOUR HEAD IN.

WARNING: consumption of alcohol may cause you to thay shings like thish.

WARNING: consumption of alcohol may lead you to believe that ex-lovers are really dying for you to telephone them at 4 in the morning.

WARNING: consumption of alcohol may leave you wondering what the hell happened to your trousers.

WARNING: consumption of alcohol may cause you to roll over in the morning and see something really scary (whose species and/or name you can't remember).

WARNING: consumption of alcohol is the leading cause of inexplicable carpet burns on the forehead.

WARNING: consumption of alcohol may create the illusion that you are tougher, handsomer and cleverer than some really, really big bloke named Wayne.

WARNING: consumption of alcohol may lead you to believe you are invisible.

WARNING: consumption of alcohol may lead you to think people are laughing WITH you.

WARNING: consumption of alcohol may cause an imbalance in the time-space continuum, whereby small (and sometimes large) gaps of time may seem to literally disappear.

*****

The little girl was SO proud of her Christmas presents, her first watch and her first perfume. She really made a pest of herself throughout the morning, going up to all the family members and sticking that watch in their ear and insisting that they smell her perfume.

Her grandparents were coming for lunch, but before their arrival, the girl's mother had said: 'If you mention that watch or that perfume just once more, I'm going to send you to your room for the rest of the day.'

The meal went rather well, and the little girl held her tongue until just when the dessert was being served. She wanted to make sure that her grandparents, too, knew about her new watch and her perfume: 'If you hear anything or smell anything . . . it's me!'

*****

Everything that used to be a sin is now a disease.

Mummy has told her little girl all about the making of babies.

Little Annie is now silent for a while.

'Do you understand it now?' Mummy asks.

'Yes,' replies her daughter.

'Do you still have any questions?'

'Yes, how about little kittens? How does that work?'

'In exactly the same way as with babies.'

'Wow!' the girl exclaims. 'My daddy can do ANYTHING!'

*****

I couldn't wait for success, so I went ahead without it.

*****

My wife and I were expecting our first child.

We were at our first antenatal examination with the middle-aged midwife. A nice woman, but she had seen it all, heard it all a million times.

I was stuttering around searching for the right words to ask when we 'should stop . . . you know . . . er, relations?'

The midwife's answer was priceless: 'Young man, as long as you don't get in my way in the delivery room, I don't care!'

*****

Two older women, Jenny and Monica, who were rivals in the same social circle, met at a party.

'My dear,' said Monica, 'are those real pearls?'

'They are,' replied Jenny.

'Of course the only way I could tell would be for me to bite them,' smiled Monica.

Jenny responded: 'Yes, but for that you would need real teeth.'

THE TOP 14 UNPUBLISHED 'BEATLES' SONGS

14. Got to Get You Off of My Wife
13. She Came In Thru John's Fragile Ego
12. She's A Woman (Who Was A Man)
11. Can't Buy Me Love (But Can Rent It By The Hour For 300 Big Ones!)
10. Polythene Pam Anderson
9. Crackbird
8. Lucy In The Sky With Linus
7. Eleanor Furby
6. All You Need Is Drugs
5. Nor-Region Woody
4. She Came In Through The White House Window
3. While My Guitar Gently Fetches £150,000 At Auction
2. I Wanna Hold You, Hans

And Topfive.com's Number 1 Unpublished Beatles Song:
1. Lay Me, Madonna

*****

This Army sergeant-major, completely frazzled by the ineptitude of his new recruits, burst into a blue streak of swearing hot enough to blister paint. He broke off suddenly when he noticed one of the young soldiers had been talking in the ranks.

'WHAT WAS THAT YOU SAID, RECRUIT??' the sergeant-major shouted.

In a quivering voice, the soldier replied: 'I said, to myself . . . Sergeant-Major sir, "If that idiot thinks I'm going to stand here and take his crap . . . well, he's certainly an uncanny judge of character."'

After years listening to his wife's pleading, this rich old farmer finally went with her to the local church on Sunday morning. He was so moved by the vicar's sermon that on the way out he stopped to shake his hand.

He said: 'Reverend, that was the best damn sermon I ever heard!'

The vicar replied: 'Oh!! Thank you, but please, I'd appreciate it if you didn't swear in the Lord's house.'

The man said: 'I'm sorry, Reverend, but I can't help myself, it was such a damn good sermon!'

The Reverend said: 'PLEASE, I cannot have you behaving this way in church!'

The man said: 'Okay, Reverend, but I just wanted you to know that I thought it was so damn good, I put a cheque for £5,000 in the collection plate.'

And the Reverend said: 'NO SHIT?'

*****

Q: What's the most common cause of hearing loss amongst men?

A: Wife saying she wants to talk to him.

*****

President Clinton said one of the toughest things about Hillary's campaign for the New York Senate was having to listen to people criticise her.

'I simply can't stand that kind of disrespect,' said the President. 'If one of my mistresses starts talking trash about Hillary, I tell them that if they are going to talk like that, they can just put their clothes on and catch a cab.'

Just to be sure it doesn't happen again, Andrew Lloyd-Webber and the entire cast of 'Cats' will be spayed or neutered.

*****

A legal secretary, a trainee solicitor and a partner in a city law firm are walking through a park on their way to lunch when they find an antique oil lamp. They rub it and a genie comes out in a puff of smoke. The genie says: 'I usually only grant three wishes, so I'll give each of you just one.'

'Me first! Me first!' says the secretary. 'I want to be in the Bahamas, driving a speedboat, without a care in the world.'

Poof! She's gone.

'Me next! Me next!' says the trainee solicitor. 'I want to be in Hawaii, relaxing on the beach with my personal masseuse, an endless supply of pina colada and the love of my life.'

Poof! He's gone.

'You're next,' the genie says to the partner.

The partner says: 'I want those two back in the office after lunch.'

*****

One day a man spotted a lamp by the roadside. He picked it up, rubbed it vigorously, and a genie appeared.

'I'll grant you your fondest wish,' the genie said.

The man thought for a moment, then said: 'I want a spectacular job — a job that no man has ever succeeded at or has ever attempted to do.'

'Poof!' said the genie. 'You're a housewife.'

The Vatican has opened a fully-outfitted and authorised Chapel in Rome's International Airport.

'Forgive me, Father, for I have sinned. It will be six minutes before my next departure.'

*****

A new book by French astronomer Pierre Kohler claims not only that astronauts have had sex in space, but also that it was part of an official NASA experiment.

'Yes, baby, it's one small organ for a man, but it's a giant snake for mankind.'

*****

I was in Birmingham a short while ago, and had a very amusing experience. While I was getting petrol, two young women in a convertible pulled in. They pulled up next to us and asked us where the lighthouses were.

'Lighthouses?' I asked.

'Yes, lighthouses. We are new to Birmingham and just can't seem to find them,' the driver replied.

Curious, and knowing that Birmingham is nowhere near the sea, I asked: 'Why are you looking for lighthouses?'

'Oh, there are so many good paying jobs for lighthouses here in the paper. But most want you to appear in person,' the passenger answered while pointing to several ads.

I stopped filling my petrol tank and walked over to see the ads. You can imagine their disappointment when I read the ads and explained that they were for 'light housekeeping'.'

A young man, hired by a supermarket, reported for his first day at work. The manager greeted him with a warm handshake and a smile, gave him a broom and said: 'Your first job will be to sweep out the store.'

'But I'm a university graduate,' the young man replied indignantly.

'Oh, I'm sorry, I didn't know that,' said the manager. 'Here, give me the broom, I'll show you how.'

*****

A policeman waited outside a busy pub, hoping to catch someone drink driving.

At closing time everyone came out and he spotted his potential quarry. The man was so obviously inebriated that he could barely walk. He stumbled around the car park for a few minutes, looking for his car.

After trying his keys on five other cars, he finally found his own vehicle. He sat in the car a good 10 minutes, as the other patrons left. He turned his lights on, then off, wipers on, then off. He started to pull forward into the grass, then stopped.

Finally, when he was the last car, he pulled out onto the road and started to drive away.

The policeman, waiting for this, turned on his lights and pulled the man over. He administered the breathalyser test, and to his great surprise, the man blew a zero.

The policeman was dumbfounded. 'This equipment must be broken!' he exclaimed.

'I doubt it,' said the man. 'Tonight was my turn to be the designated decoy!'

Bumper Stickers:

If You Don't Believe In Oral Sex, Keep Your Mouth Shut.

If You Can Read This, I've Lost My Caravan.

This Would Be Really Funny If It Weren't Happening To Me!

I'm Cleverly Disguised As A Responsible Adult.

If We Stop Voting Will They All Go Away?

The Face Is Familiar But I Can't Quite Remember My Name ...

It's Been Lovely But I Have To Scream Now.

I Haven't Lost My Mind, It's Backed Up On Disk Somewhere.

If Walking Is So Good For You, Then Why Does My Postman Look Like Jabba The Hutt?

Caution — Driver Legally Blonde!

Don't Be Sexist — Birds Hate That.

How Many Roads Must A Man Travel Down Before He Admits He Is Lost?

Another story from America. Seems this hillbilly came to town carrying a jug of moonshine in one hand and a shotgun in the other. He stopped a man on the street, saying to him: 'Here, friend, take a drink outta my jug.'

The man protested, saying he never drank.

Unimpressed, the hillbilly levelled his shotgun at the stranger and commanded: 'Drink!'

The stranger drank, shuddered, shook, shivered and coughed.

'God! That's awful stuff!'

'Ain't it, though?' replied the hillbilly. 'Now here, you hold the gun on me and make me take a swig.'

*****

Those of you who have ever heard native Texas girls speak know they're really slow talkers.

Usually that's not a problem.

Unless, of course, they're trying to convince some guy they're not that kind of girl.

See, by the time they're halfway finished — they are.

*****

Cheryl's mum is disgusted with talk about condoms and the word itself isn't in her vocabulary. She phoned Cheryl and told her: 'I'm so sick of those ads for those "thingies". I'm telling you they're EVERYWHERE. Honestly, I went through a drive-thru at McDonald's and they were giving them away at the window!!!'

Cheryl corrected her and said: 'Mummy, the sign was CONDIMENTS, not CONDOMS.'

JUDI THE BIMBO . . .

Judi has been working as a secretary at a new firm for a week when her boss tells her: 'I'll tell you a little secret. I can read your mind!'

'Really?' says Judi.

'Yes,' replies the boss, as he looks deep into her eyes. For instance, I know you've had a date with a man called Bob last Tuesday.'

'WOW!' exclaims Judi. 'Unbelievable! That's true!'

'And,' continues the boss, 'your Mum's birthday is 22 April.'

'Amazing!' says Judi. 'I can't believe it! You really CAN read my mind!'

'Well actually' her boss says, 'you left your private diary in my room yesterday.'

'Fantastic!' says Judi. 'You even know THAT!'

*****

Karen had Judi as a customer once. Judi was trying to return a battery-operated wrist-watch that she'd bought 18 months earlier. She said it didn't work. Karen suggested that all she needed was a new battery.

Judi replied: 'You don't get it! The battery shouldn't be dead because I hardly ever WEAR this watch!'

*****

Reg was driving a whole busload of Judies home past a well-known gay nightclub in London's Soho one night. There was a line of men to get in, even at 2:15am, and one Judi in the back commented: 'If it's so popular, why aren't there any women waiting to get in?'

'X' tells me he employed Judi when she was 18. She'd complained that someone had mistaken her for 14. He replied that he'd had a 'five-year-old' working for him once. She tried to work it out: 'Was it one of those "bring your child to work" things?' Finally 'X' told her that the 'five-year-old' had had 29th February as a birthday and had only celebrated five birthdays.

Judi swore she'd never heard of such a thing and actually asked: 'So . . . did she . . . not "age", then?'

*****

Finally, Judith turns herself into a Judi. She'd been in the habit of stumbling to her computer first thing in the morning to read the news. One morning she was especially aggravated at the slow pace and growled out: 'Why doesn't someone just invent something that you can turn on and it TELLS you the news???' That's when she glanced eight feet away at that device called a 'television'.

*****

A car breaks down on the motorway one day, so the driver eases it over onto the hard shoulder.

He jumps out of the car, opens the boot, and pulls out two men in trench coats.

The men stand behind the car, open up their coats and start exposing themselves to the oncoming traffic. This results in one of the worst pile-ups in history.

When questioned by police why he put two deviants along the side of the road, the man replies: 'I broke down and was just using my emergency flashers!'

An old farmer is outside for a walk around his land when he sees a sign on his neighbour's lawn: 'Horse for Sale'. Curious, he decides to have a look. As he approaches his neighbour's stable, he sees his old Italian friend brushing down a fine-looking stallion.

'Hello, friend, I saw your sign out there and came over to see your horse for sale.'

Now, the Italian farmer speaks very poor English, but manages to answer well enough: 'Yep, yep, disa is da horse fora sale.'

'This horse here?' quizzes the old farmer. 'Why, he's a fine horse! Why ever would you sell him?'

'Well,' sighs the Italian farmer, 'he no looka so good anymore.'

The old farmer, convinced that his neighbour has lost his mind, makes the sale and leads the horse across his field over to the stable. As he taps the horse gently on the back to coax him into the stable, he watches as the horse misses the door completely and smacks head first into the wall. 'That old cheat sold me a blind horse!' growls the old farmer. He then proceeds to storm over across the field, reins in hand, to give his neighbour a piece of his mind. 'You sold me a blind horse, you old cheat, and you didn't even tell me!' he screams.

'Eh! I tolla you!' cries the Italian farmer. 'I say: "he no looka so good anymore!" '

*****

Before we were married my wife always used to say: 'You're only interested in one thing.' The trouble is now though, after 36 years, I've forgotten what the hell it was.

Things you don't want to hear during surgery:

1. 'Oops.'
2. 'Damn, I forgot my glasses again.'
3. 'Oh no, not again.'
4. 'Hey, bring that back!! Bad dog. A human bone is no toy for a dog!'
5. 'Someone call the cleaner, we have a BIG mess again.'
6. 'Damn, I can't get my arm out of her back. We're going to have to cut it off.'
7. 'And now we place the ape's brain in the subject's body.'
8. 'That's interesting! Can you make his leg twitch?'
9. 'What? They're missing that too? Oh well, I suppose we'll have to try to remember how to do surgery.'
10. 'What do you mean, he wasn't in for a sex change?'
11. 'Oops. Hey, has anyone ever survived 500ml of this stuff before?'
12. 'You know, there's big money in kidneys. Look, this one's got two of them.'
13. 'Could you stop that thing from thumping, it's disturbing my concentration.'
14. 'You forgot what he was in for? Oh well, let's surprise him.'
15. 'Accept this sacrifice, O Great Lord of Darkness.'
16. 'Wait a minute. If this is his spleen, then what's that?'
17. 'Hand me that . . . er . . . that er . . . thingie.'
18. 'Um, is this thing supposed to be moving? Because I think it's about to choke the patient.'

*****

We're fifty billion pounds in debt as a country. Who do we owe this money to?

FIFTEEN GREAT THINGS ABOUT GETTING OLDER

1. You can eat dinner at 4pm.
2. Your investment in private health care is finally over.
3. If you've never smoked, you can start now, and it won't begin to cause you any harm.
4. Kidnappers are not very interested in you.
5. It's harder and harder for sexual harassment charges to have time to hurt you.
6. People no longer view you as a hypochondriac.
7. Your secrets are safe with your friends as they can no longer remember them.
8. Your supply of brain cells is now down to a manageable size.
9. Your eyes won't get much worse.
10. Adult nappies are actually quite convenient.
11. Things you buy now won't wear out.
12. No one expects you to run into a burning building.
13. There's nothing left to learn the hard way.
14. Your joints are more accurate than the Met Office.
15. In a hostage situation you are likely to be released first.

*****

Personal Ad Of The Week:
I'm Filthy, Stinking, Rich.
Well, Two Out of Three Ain't Bad

*****

Best 'Pulling line' of all time!
'I'm single, with two million pounds, but I've got a weak heart.'

This has got to be one of the funniest stories I've heard in a long time. I think this person should have been promoted, not fired**.**

This is a true story from the WordPerfect Helpline . It was transcribed from a recording monitoring the customer care department. Needless to say the Help Desk employee was fired; however, he/she is currently suing the WordPerfect organisation for 'Wrongful dismissal' or as they say in America 'Termination without Cause'.

Actual dialogue of a former WordPerfect Customer Support employee (now I know why they record these conversations!):

'Ridge Hall computer assistance; may I help you?'

'Yes, well, I'm having trouble with WordPerfect.'

'What sort of trouble?'

'Well, I was just typing along, and all of a sudden the words went away.'

'Went away?'

'They disappeared.'

'Hmm. So what does your screen look like now?'

'Nothing.'

'Nothing?'

'It's blank; it won't accept anything when I type.'

'Are you still in WordPerfect, or did you get out?'

'How do I tell?'

'Can you see the C: prompt on the screen?'

'What's a sea-prompt?'

'Never mind, can you move your cursor around the screen?'

'There isn't any cursor: I told you, it won't accept anything I type.'

'Does your monitor have a power indicator?'

'What's a monitor?'

'It's the thing with the screen on it that looks like a TV. Does it have a little light that tells you when it's on?'

'I don't know.'

'Well, then look on the back of the monitor and find where the power cord goes into it. Can you see that?'

'Yes, I think so.'

'Great. Follow the cord to the plug, and tell me if it's plugged into the wall.'

'Yes, it is.'

'When you were behind the monitor, did you notice that there were two cables plugged into the back of it, not just one?'

'No.'

'Well, there are. I need you to look back there again and find the other cable.'

'Okay, here it is.'

'Follow it for me, and tell me if it's plugged securely into the back of your computer.'

'I can't reach.'

'OK. Well, can you see if it is?'

'No.'

'Even if you maybe put your knee on something and lean way over?'

'Oh, it's not because I don't have the right angle — it is because it's dark.'

'Dark?'

'Yes — the office light is off, and the only light I have is coming in from the window.'

'Well, turn on the office light then.'

'I can't.'

'No? Why not?'

'Because there's a power failure.'

'A power . . . A power failure? Aha. Okay, we've got it sorted now. Do you still have the boxes and manuals and packing stuff your computer came in?'

'Well, yes, I keep them in the cupboard.'

'Good. Go and get them, and unplug your system and pack it

up just like it was when you got it. Then take it back to the shop you bought it from.'

'Really? Is it that bad?'

'Yes, I'm afraid it is.'

'Well, all right then, I suppose. What do I tell them?'

'Tell them you're too bloody stupid to own a computer.'

*****

'I wish I was a glow worm
A glow worm's never glum
Cos how can you be grumpy
When the sun shines out your bum'

*****

A man wakes up in the morning. He has a massive hangover and can't remember anything he did last night.

He picks up his dressing gown from the floor and puts it on. He notices there's something in one of the pockets and it turns out to be a bra.

He thinks: Bloody hell what happened last night??

He walks towards the bathroom and finds a pair of knickers in the other pocket of his dressing gown. Again he thinks: What happened last night? Who was I with? Must have been a wild party.

He opens the bathroom door, walks in and has a look in the mirror. He notices a little string hanging out of his mouth and his only thought is: If there's a god, please let this be a teabag.

These are the nominees for the Vauxhall 'NOVA' Award for Marketing. This is given out in honour of the General Motors fiasco in trying to market the Nova model car in Central and South America. '*No va*' means, of course, in Spanish, 'it doesn't go'.

1. The US Dairy Association's huge success with the campaign 'Got Milk?' prompted it to expand advertising to Mexico. It was soon brought to its attention that the Spanish translation read: 'Are you lactating?'

2. Coors — beers — put its slogan, 'Turn It Loose', into Spanish, where it was read as 'Suffer from diarrhoea'.

3. Scandinavian vacuum cleaner manufacturer Electrolux used the following in an American campaign:
   'Nothing sucks like an Electrolux.'

4. Clairol introduced the 'Mist Stick', a curling iron, into Germany only to find out that '*Mist*' is slang for manure. Not too many people had use for the 'Manure Stick'.

5. When Gerber started selling baby food in Africa, it used the same packaging as in the US, with the smiling baby on the label. Later it learned that in Africa companies routinely put pictures on the labels of what's inside, since many people can't read.

6. Colgate introduced a toothpaste in France called Cue, the name of a notorious porno magazine.

7. An American T-shirt maker in Miami printed shirts for the Spanish market which promoted the Pope's visit. Instead of 'I saw the Pope' (*el Papa*), the shirts read 'I saw the potato' (*la papa*).

8. Pepsi's 'Come Alive With the Pepsi Generation' translated into 'Pepsi Brings Your Ancestors Back From the Grave' in Chinese.

9. The Coca-Cola name in China was first read as '*kekoukela*', meaning 'bite the wax tadpole' or 'female horse stuffed with wax', depending on the dialect. Coke then researched 40,000 characters to find a phonetic equivalent '*kokou kole*', translating into 'happiness in the mouth'.

10. Frank Perdue's chicken slogan: 'It takes a strong man to make a tender chicken' was translated into Spanish as 'it takes an aroused man to make a chicken affectionate'.

11. When Parker Pen marketed a ball-point pen in Mexico, its ads were supposed to have read: 'It won't leak in your pocket and embarrass you.'
  The company thought that the word '*embarazar*' (to impregnate) meant 'to embarrass', so the ad read: 'It won't leak in your pocket and make you pregnant'!

12. When American Airlines wanted to advertise its new leather first class seats in the Mexican market, it translated its 'Fly In Leather' campaign literally, which meant 'Fly Naked' (*vuela en cuero*) in Spanish!

13. Recently the fast food chain Kentucky Fried Chicken has been running advertisements for its new buffet. In the television commercials, various store personnel sing the praises of the buffet. They are not particularly good singers, and the song is rather pathetic. The whole thing appears to have been done in jest. This commercial is generally recognised (ie, by a few of my friends and me) as one of the worst in recent memory.
  It seems that one American KFC outlet recognises this as

well. Recently the sign outside this particular store read (I am NOT making this up):

'Try Our New Buffet — Or We'll Run The Commercial Again'

*****

Little boy to his mother: 'Mummy, am I descended from a monkey?'
The mother replied: 'I don't know, son, I never met your father's family.'

*****

'How does Janice like being pregnant?' Bob asked his friend John.
'Oh, she's not pregnant,' John replied, 'she's expecting.'
'What's the difference?' Bob pressed.
'Well, John explained, 'she's expecting me to cook dinner, she's expecting me to do the housework, she's expecting me to rub her feet . . .'

*****

Is there a man alive who hasn't had this conversation — at least in his own head?
   Woman: 'Are you good in bed?'
   Man: 'Of course I am.'
   Woman: 'How do you know?'
   Man: 'Because I'm always satisfied.'

An airline captain was breaking in a very pretty new blonde stewardess. The route they were flying had a stop-over in another city. Upon their arrival the captain showed the stewardess the best place for airline personnel to eat, shop and stay overnight.

The next morning as the pilot was preparing the crew for the day's route, he noticed the new stewardess was missing. He knew which room she was in at the hotel and called her up wondering what happened to her.

She answered the phone, crying, and said she couldn't get out of her room.

'You can't get out of your room?' the captain asked. 'Why not?'

The stewardess sobbed in reply: 'There are only three doors in here. One is the bathroom, one is the toilet, and one has a sign on it that says "Do Not Disturb"!'

*****

ROMANCE

He put his hand around my neck,
So that I could not scream.
He brought me up to his room,
So we would not be seen.
He took off all my wrappings,
And gazed upon my form.
As I stood cold and shivering,
He stood there hot and warm.
He touched me with his feverish lips,
And placed me on my rear.
He made me what I am today,
An empty bottle of beer.

After a long, bumpy flight, our passengers were glad to finally land. They disembarked, and the other attendants and I checked for items left behind.

In a seat pocket, I found a bag of home-made cookies with a note saying: 'Much love, Mummy'. Quickly, I gave the bag to our gate agent in hopes it would be reunited with its owner.

A few minutes later, this announcement came over the public-address system in the concourse:

'Would the passenger who lost his cookies on Flight 502, please return to the gate?'

*****

Some tourists in the Natural History Museum are marvelling at the dinosaur bones. One of them asks the attendant: 'Can you tell me how old the dinosaur bones are?'

The attendant replies: 'They are three million, four years, and six months old.'

'That's an awfully exact number,' says the tourist. 'How do you know their age so precisely?'

The attendant answers: 'Well, the dinosaur bones were three million years old when I started working here, and that was four and a half years ago.'

*****

Two friends were out drinking when suddenly one lurched backward off his barstool and lay motionless on the floor. 'One thing about Jim,' his mate said to the barman, 'he knows when to stop.'

David received a parrot for his birthday.

The parrot was fully grown with a bad attitude and worse vocabulary.

Every other word was an expletive.

Those that weren't expletives were, to say the least, very rude.

David tried hard to change the bird's attitude and was constantly saying polite words, playing soft music, anything he could think of to try to set a good example. Nothing worked.

He yelled at the bird and the bird yelled back.

He shook the bird and the bird just got more angry and became even more rude.

Finally, in a moment of desperation, David put the parrot in the freezer.

For a few moments he heard the bird squawk and kick and scream.

Then suddenly, there was quiet — not a sound for half a minute.

David was frightened that he might have hurt the bird and quickly opened the freezer door.

The parrot calmly stepped out onto David's extended arm and said: 'I believe I may have offended you with my rude language and actions. I will endeavour at once to correct my behaviour. I really am truly sorry and beg your forgiveness.'

David was astonished at the bird's change in attitude and was about to ask what had made such a dramatic change when the parrot continued: 'May I ask what the chicken did?'

*****

I was microwaving something the other day, and it had this notice on it:

'WARNING: hot when heated.'

I'm so racked with guilt. I don't want to stop therapy because I'm afraid to take the income away from my therapist.

He's got children at university.

*****

A man walks through the front door of a pub. He is obviously drunk, and staggers up to the bar, seats himself on a stool and, with a belch, asks the barman for a drink. The barman politely informs the man that as it appears that he has already had plenty to drink, he could not be served additional alcohol at this pub, and could a taxi be called for him?

The drunk is briefly surprised, then softly scoffs, grumbles, climbs down off the bar stool and staggers out of the front door. A few minutes later, the same drunk stumbles in the SIDE door of the pub. He wobbles up to the bar and calls for a drink. The barman comes over and, still politely — but more firmly — refuses service to the man due to his inebriation, and again offers to call a taxi. The drunk looks at the barman for a moment angrily, swears, and shows himself out of the side door, all the while grumbling and shaking his head.

A few minutes later, the same drunk bursts in through the BACK door of the pub. He props himself up on a bar stool, gathers his wits and belligerently orders a drink. The barman comes over and emphatically reminds the man that he is clearly drunk, will be served no drinks, and either a taxi or the police will be called immediately.

The surprised drunk looks at the barman, and in hopeless anguish, cries: 'MAAAN! How many pubs do you work at?'

The attractive young thing was about to go to bed with her blind date when she burst into tears.

'I'm afraid you'll get the wrong idea about me,' she said between sobs. 'I'm really not that kind of girl!'

'I believe you,' her date said, as he tried to comfort her.

'You're the first one,' she gulped.

'The first one to make love to you?' he asked.

'No!' she replied. 'The first one to believe me.'

*****

A woman went to the doctor's surgery and said: 'Doctor, I've got a bit of a problem. But, I'll have to take my clothes off to show you.' The doctor told her to go behind the screen and disrobe.

She did and the doctor went around to see her when she was ready.

'Well, what is it?' he asked.

'It's a bit embarrassing,' she replied. 'These two green circles have appeared on the inside of my thighs.'

The doctor examined her and finally admitted he had no idea what the cause was.

Suddenly, the doctor asked: 'Does your boyfriend wear earrings?'

'Why, yes, doctor, he does.'

'Tell him they're not real gold.'

*****

Before you criticise someone, walk a mile in his shoes. Then when you do criticise that person, you'll be a mile away and have his shoes.

Jill: 'So, Lynne, how's your sex life these days?'
Lynne: 'Oh, you know. It's the usual, Social Security kind.'
Jill: 'Social Security?'
Lynne: 'Yes, you get a little each month, but it's not enough to live on.'

*****

After an overnight flight to meet my father at his latest military posting, my mother wearily arrived at the airbase in Germany with my eight siblings and me — all under the age of 11.

Collecting our many suitcases, the 10 of us entered the cramped customs area. A young customs official watched our entourage in disbelief: 'Ma'am,' he said, 'do all these children and this luggage belong to you?'

'Yes,' my mother said with a sigh. 'They're all mine.'

The customs agent began his interrogation: 'Ma'am, do you have any weapons, contraband or illegal drugs in your possession?'

She calmly answered: 'If I'd had any of those items, I would have used them by now.'

*****

I've been in love with the same woman for 41 years. If my wife finds out, she'll kill me.

*****

Life is something you do when you can't get to sleep.

A group of senior citizens were exchanging notes about their ailments:

'My arm is so weak I can hardly hold this coffee cup.'

'Yes, I know. My cataracts are so bad I can't see to pour the coffee.'

'I can't turn my head because of the arthritis in my neck.'

'My blood pressure pills make me dizzy.'

'I suppose that's the price we pay for getting old.'

'Well, it's not all bad. We should be thankful that we can still drive!'

*****

Frank came up to his wife one day. 'If I were, say, disfigured, would you still love me?' he asked her.

'Darling, I'll always love you,' she said calmly, filing her nails.

'How about if I became crippled and couldn't make love to you any more?' he asked nervously.

'Don't worry, darling, I'll always love you,' she told him, buffing her nails.

'Well, how about if I lost my job as vice president?' Frank went on. 'If I weren't pulling in six figures any more. Would you still love me then?'

The woman looked over at her husband's worried face. 'Frank, I'll always love you,' she reassured him, 'but most of all, I'll really miss you.'

One day in the Garden of Eden, Eve calls out to God . . .
'Lord, I have a problem!'
'What's the problem, Eve?'
'Lord, I know you've created me and have provided this beautiful garden and all of these wonderful animals, and that hilarious comedic snake, but I'm just not happy.'
'Why is that, Eve?' comes the reply from above.
'Lord, I am lonely. And I'm sick to death of apples.'
'Well, Eve, in that case, I have a solution. I shall create a man for you.'
'What's a "man", Lord?'
'This man will be a flawed creature, with many bad traits. He'll lie, cheat, and be vainglorious; all in all, he'll give you a hard time. But, he'll be bigger, faster, and will like to hunt and kill things. He will look silly aroused, but since you've been complaining, I'll create him in such a way that he will satisfy your, er, physical needs. He'll be witless and will revel in childish things like fighting and kicking a ball about. He won't be too clever, so he'll also need your advice to think properly.'
'Sounds great,' says Eve, with an ironically raised eyebrow.
'What's the catch, Lord?'
'Well . . . You can have him on one condition.'
'What's that, Lord?'
'As I said, he'll be proud, arrogant, and self-admiring . . . So you'll have to let him believe that I made him first . . . So, just remember . . . it's our secret . . . Woman to woman!'

*****

A reader wrote to me and told me he recently got a prescription for 'Zolpidem' — a type of sleeping pill. He said: 'Funny, on the warning label it states: "May cause drowsiness".'

A flock of sheep is grazing in a field. The sheep are happily going 'baa baa' to each other and discussing life as usual when suddenly they hear a 'moo mooooooooooooooooooooo!'

They look around and see only sheep. They carry on grazing as before.

'Moooooo moooooooooooo mmmoo!'

One sheep can hear it all too clearly next to her. She shuffles away a little from her friend, a worried look on her face and then asks: 'Georgina, why are you mooing? You're a sheep. Sheep go "baa!"'

Her friend replies gladly: 'I know, I just thought I would learn a foreign language!'

*****

I work in a busy office where a computer going down causes quite an inconvenience. Recently one of our computers not only crashed, it made a noise that sounded like a heart monitor. 'This computer has flat-lined,' a colleague called out with mock horror.

'Does anyone here know how to do mouse-to-mouse resuscitation?'

*****

Little Johnny was eating breakfast one morning and got to thinking about things. 'Mummy, mummy, why has daddy got so few hairs on his head?' he asked his mother.

'He thinks a lot,' replied his mother, pleased with herself for coming up with a good answer to her husband's baldness.

Or she was until Johnny thought for a second and asked: 'So why do you have so much hair?'

Another story from America. A couple arrived at the Chicago town hall seconds before closing time, and caught a judge just as he was about to leave, and asked him to marry them. He asked if they had a licence and, when they didn't, sent them off to get one.

They caught the town clerk just as he was locking up, and got the licence from him. When they got back to the judge, he pointed out they had filled the names in backwards — his where hers belonged and vice versa.

They rushed back to the clerk's office, caught him again, and got another licence. This time, the judge noticed that the clerk had filled in the date in the wrong format. Again they caught the clerk . . . After five reissued licences, the judge was finally satisfied.

Judge: 'I hope you appreciate why I made you keep going back. If there are irregularities in the licence, your marriage would not be legal, and any children you might have would be technical bastards.'

Groom: 'That's funny — that's just what the clerk called you.'

*****

Two Irishmen rob a bank and all they get away with are two sacks, so they keep one each. After a while they meet again and one asks the other: 'What did you find in your sack?'

'Half a million.'

'That's a lot! What did you do with the cash?'

'I bought a house. How about your sack?'

'It was full of bills.'

'And what did you do with them?'

'Eh well . . . little by little, I'm paying them off . . .'

The central operations department of a large bank is connected by a computer network to all the bank's branch offices. Much important information is stored in the head office computer, and is always available to every branch — always, that is, unless the system goes down. Then it's anybody's guess as to when they can get it to start working again.

In other words, all the branches are tied to the central office, and everybody depends on the central computer.

One day a woman called from one of the branches, and she sounded very concerned.

She said: 'There's smoke coming from the back of my terminal. Do you guys have a fire in your offices?'

*****

A gentleman had been trying for years to meet the Pope.

Finally, his wish was granted. When the gentleman approached the Pope he said: 'Your Eminence, I am so happy to be given this chance to speak with you and I would like to tell you a joke before I start.'

The Pope replied: 'Of course, my son. Go ahead and tell your joke.'

The gentleman continued: 'There were these two Polacks and —'

The Pope interrupted: 'My son, do you realise that I am Polish?'

'I'm sorry, Your Holiness, I'll speak slower . . .'

*****

The caption under a cartoon showing a doctor handing a couple of pills to his patient: 'Take one of these tonight and the other IF you wake up in the morning.'

Sam was worried. His teenage daughter was hitch-hiking home from London to Liverpool by herself.

She was 17 but was built like she was 25.

When she arrived home unscathed, her father was curious as to how she avoided men hassling her — and worse!

'I simply told the men who picked me up that I was going to Liverpool because they have the best AIDS clinic in the country,' she replied sweetly.

*****

A vicar visiting the local church school asks little Johnny during RE who broke down the walls of Jericho. Little Johnny replies that he does not know, but it definitely was not him.

The vicar, taken aback by this lack of basic Bible knowledge, goes to the headmaster and relates the whole incident.

The headmaster replies that he knows little Johnny and his whole family very well and can vouch for them; if little Johnny said that he did not do it, he as headmaster is satisfied that it is the truth.

Even more appalled, the vicar goes to the local Head of Education and relates the whole story.

After listening he replies: 'I cannot see why you are making such a big issue out of this; we will get three quotations and fix the damned wall.'

*****

Q: You know what's the really nice thing about having Alzheimer's disease?

A: You're ALWAYS meeting new people.

The waitress was tired of this one customer always harassing her, so she came up with a plan. 'I'll tell you what, stud. I'll have sex with you on two conditions.

'First, it'll cost you £50. Second, you have to guarantee me that bells will ring and lights will flash.'

He smiled, handed her £50 and led her over to the pinball machine.

*****

Miss Jones had been giving her young students a lesson on science. She had explained about magnets and showed how they would pick up nails and other bits of iron.

Now it was question time and she asked: 'My name begins with the letter "M" and I pick up things. What am I?'

A little boy on the front row said: 'You're a mother.'

*****

As a little girl climbed onto Santa's lap, Santa asked the usual: 'And what would you like for Christmas?'

The child stared at him open-mouthed and horrified for a minute, then gasped: 'Didn't you get my E-mail?'

*****

'Pilot to control tower . . . pilot to control tower . . . I am 300 miles from land . . . 600 feet over water . . . and running out of fuel . . . please instruct!'

'Tower to pilot . . . tower to pilot . . . repeat after me: "Our Father, which art in heaven . . ."'

One night, torrential rain soaked Christchurch in Dorset. The next morning the resulting floodwaters came up about 6ft into most of the homes there.

Mrs Ramsey was sitting on her roof with her neighbour, Mrs Greenly, waiting for help to come.

Mrs Greenly noticed a lone baseball cap floating near the house. Then she saw it float far out into the back garden, then float all the way back to the house. It kept floating away from the house, then back in.

Her curiosity got the better of her, so she asked Mrs Ramsey: 'Do you see that baseball cap floating away from the house, then back again?'

Mrs Ramsey said: 'Oh yes, that's my husband; I told him he was going to cut the grass today come hell or high water!'

*****

A new priest is nervous about hearing confessions, so he asks an older priest to sit in on his sessions.

The new priest hears a couple of confessions, then the old priest asks him to step out of the confessional for a few suggestions.

The old priest suggests: 'Cross your arms over your chest, and rub your chin with one hand.' The new priest tries this.

The old priest suggests: 'Try saying things like: "I see, yes, go on", and "I understand. How did you feel about that?"'

The new priest says those things, trying them out. The old priest says: 'Now, don't you think that's a little better than slapping your knee and saying: "No way! What happened next?"'

Fred was drinking in the pub and the barman came over to tell him he had a telephone call. Fred had just bought another beer and he didn't want anyone to drink it. So, Fred wrote a little sign and left it by his beer that said:

'I spat in my beer.'

When Fred returned to his bar stool there was another note beside his beer:

'So did I.'

*****

A car stalled on a country lane. When the driver got out to fix it, a cow came along and stopped beside him. 'Your trouble is probably in the carburettor,' said the cow.

Startled, the man jumped back and ran down the road until he met the farmer. He told the farmer his story.

'Was it a large red cow with a brown spot over the right eye?' asked the farmer.

'Yes!'

'Oh, I wouldn't listen to Bessie,' said the farmer. 'She doesn't know anything about cars.'

*****

A knight and his men return to their castle after a hard month of riding.

'How are we faring?' his king asks.

'Sire,' replies the knight, 'I have been robbing and pillaging on your behalf all day, burning the towns of your enemies in the west.'

'What?!' shrieks the king. 'I don't have any enemies to the west!'

'Oh,' replies the knight. 'Well, you do now.'

Stevie Wonder and Tiger Woods are in a bar. Woods turns to Wonder and says: 'How is the singing career going?'

Stevie Wonder replies: 'Not too bad! How's the golf?'

Woods replies: 'Not too bad. I've had some problems with my swing, but I think I've got that right now.'

Stevie Wonder says: 'I always find that when my swing goes wrong, I need to stop playing for a while and not think about it. Then, the next time I play, it seems to be all right.'

Tiger Woods says: 'You play golf?'

Stevie Wonder says: 'Oh, yes, I've been playing for years.'

And Woods says: 'But you're blind. How can you play golf if you're blind?'

Wonder replies: 'I get my caddy to stand in the middle of the fairway and call to me. I listen for the sound of his voice and play the ball towards him. Then, when I get to where the ball lands, the caddy moves to the green or farther down the fairway and again I play the ball towards his voice.'

'But how do you putt?' asks Woods.

'Well,' says Stevie, 'I get my caddy to lean down in front of the hole and call to me with his head on the ground and I just play the ball towards his voice.'

Woods asks: 'What's your handicap?'

Stevie says: 'Well, I'm a scratch golfer.'

Woods, incredulous, says to Stevie: 'We've got to play a round sometime.'

Wonder replies: 'Well, people don't take me seriously, so I only play for money, and never play for less than $10,000 a hole.'

Woods thinks about it and says: 'OK, I'm game for that, when would you like to play?'

Stevie says: 'Pick a night!'

A new soldier is on sentry duty at the main gate. His orders are clear. No car is to enter unless it has a special sticker on the windscreen. A big Army car comes up with a general seated in the back. The sentry says: 'Halt, who goes there?'

The chauffeur, a corporal, says: 'General Wheeler.'

'I'm sorry, I can't let you through. You've got to have a sticker on the windscreen.'

The general says: 'Drive on!'

The sentry says: 'Hold it! You really can't come through. I have orders to shoot if you try driving in without a sticker.'

The general repeats: 'I'm telling you, driver, drive on!'

The sentry walks up to the rear window and says: 'General, I'm new at this. Do I shoot you or the driver?'

*****

A man comes home from work one day and he says to his wife: 'Darling, I've got a new secretary. And imagine what happened! She's got a red and white bra. You know, these are the colours of my favourite football team. Anyway, it's not a big deal but it feels good.'

The next day when he comes home his wife asks: 'How was your day?'

The man says: 'Fantastic! It's not only her bra that is red and white but also her knickers. You know it's not a big deal but it really feels good!'

The third day they meet at home after work and now the man asks his wife: 'And what happened today in your office, darling?'

She says: 'Oh, nothing special, sweetheart. I got a new boss today. He's about two inches bigger than you. You know it's not a big deal but hell it feels good!'

A little boy returning home from his first day at school said to his mother: 'Mummy, what's sex?'

His mother, who believed in all the most modern educational theories, gave him a detailed explanation, covering all aspects of the tricky subject.

When she had finished, the little lad produced an enrolment form which he had brought home from school and said: 'Yes, but how am I going to get all that into this one little square?'

*****

Once you reach middle management, promotions are hard to come by in the office. I congratulated one woman on her recent upgrade and asked if she would mind telling me how she pulled it off.

She smiled and said: 'Well, of course. But I doubt very much if it'll do you any good.'

*****

Did you hear about the two women who were watching a blonde walk by?

The first one said: 'I wonder whether she's a natural blonde or a bleached blonde.'

Her friend said: 'She's a suicide blonde.'

The other said: 'Suicide blonde? What's that?'

The friend said: 'Dyed by her own hand!'

A farmer was helping one of his cows give birth, when he noticed his four-year-old son standing wide-eyed at the fence, soaking in the whole event. The man thought: Great . . . he's four and I'm going to have to start explaining the birds and bees. Still, no need to jump the gun — I'll just let him ask, and I'll answer.

After everything was over, the man walked over to his son and said: 'Well son, do you have any questions?'

'Just one,' gasped the still wide-eyed lad. 'How fast was that calf going when he hit that cow?'

*****

A man died and went to The Judgement. St Peter met him at the Gates of Heaven and said: 'Before you meet with God, I thought I should tell you — we've looked at your life, and you really didn't do anything particularly good or bad. We're not at all sure what to do with you. Can you tell us anything you did that can help us make a decision?'

The newly arrived soul thought for a moment and replied:

'Yes, once I was driving along and came upon a woman who was being harassed by a group of bikers. So I pulled over, got out my car jack, and went up to the leader of the bikers. He was a big, muscular, hairy guy with tattoos all over his body and a ring pierced through his nose. Well, I tore the nose ring out of his nose, and told him that he and his gang had better stop bothering the woman or they would have to deal with me!'

'I'm impressed,' St Peter responded. 'When did this happen?'

'About two minutes ago,' came the reply.

The new vicar was up early one Sunday morning, walking round his new parish after leaving his wife in bed with the Sunday papers, her cup of tea, and a pack of cigarettes.

One of the old villagers came up to him and said: 'Good morning, Vicar, how be you and the wife?'

The vicar said: 'Good morning, my man. I am fine, the wife is fine also as I left her in bed smoking.'

The villager said: 'Arr, Vicar, that's the way to love 'em!'

*****

It was mealtime during our trip on a small airline in the Northwest. 'Would you like dinner?' the flight attendant asked the man seated in front of me.

'What are the choices?' he asked.

'Yes or No,' she replied.

*****

A husband and wife walked into a restaurant and seated themselves at a vacant table. Soon, the waitress came over to take their order. '.. and to drink,' she asked. The wife didn't want one but the man said he would like a coffee.

The waitress promptly returned with a cup of coffee, but spilled it on the man's lap when she stopped at the table.

'Oh my God! I am so sorry!'

'That's OK,' the man said, sopping up the puddles on his trousers with his napkin.

Wife: 'Was that regular or decaf?'

'Regular,' she replied

'Oh great ... now he'll be up all night.'

DEEP THOUGHTS:

If they ever come up with a swashbuckling college, I think one of the courses should be Laughing, Then Jumping Off Something.

It takes a big man to cry, but it takes a bigger man to laugh at that man.

Too bad you can't buy a voodoo globe so that you could make the earth spin really fast and freak everybody out.

I don't think I'm alone when I say I'd like to see more and more planets fall under the ruthless domination of our solar system.

Dad always thought laughter was the best medicine, which I suppose is why several of us died of tuberculosis.

Maybe in order to understand mankind, we have to look at the word itself: 'Mankind'. Basically, it's made up of two separate words — 'mank' and 'ind'. What do these words mean?
   It's a mystery, and that's why is mankind also.

I hope if dogs ever take over the world, and they choose a king, they don't just go by size, because I bet there are some Chihuahuas with some good ideas.

I bet the main reason the police keep people away from a plane crash is they don't want anybody walking in and lying down in the crash stuff, then, when somebody comes up, pretend that they have just woken up and going: 'What was THAT?!'

I worry that the person who thought of Muzak may be thinking up something else.

*****

The End — I bet you thought it would never come.

*****